MAD DOG

MAD DOG

THE MICKEY LEWIS STORY

LEO ACKERMAN AND ALEX URWIN

First published by Pitch Publishing, 2025

Pitch Publishing
9 Donnington Park,
85 Birdham Road,
Chichester, West Sussex,
PO20 7AJ
www.pitchpublishing.co.uk
info@pitchpublishing.co.uk

A CIP catalogue record is available for this book
from the British Library.

ISBN 978 1 80150 936 7

Typesetting and origination by Pitch Publishing

Printed and bound on FSC® certified paper in line with
our continuing commitment to ethical business practices,
sustainability and the environment.

Printed and bound in India by Replika Press Pvt. Ltd.

Contents

Introduction

MICKEY LEWIS'S 'One for the Road' memorial match took place at the Kassam Stadium, the home of Oxford United, on Sunday, 10 October 2021.

For anyone passing the stadium that morning, tucked away as it is on a business park a short drive outside of Oxford's city centre, things might have seemed ordinary. The weather was pleasant for mid-autumn. Cold and bright, if a little moist from rain a few hours prior.

But, by late morning, there was a noticeable buzz around the players' entrance, stretching into the bowels of the stadium. Laughter carried through the walls. Old friends – a little heavier and a little greyer than they'd been on previous visits to this part of town – embraced in crowded corridors, asking after years passed, reminiscing about glory days shared in similar surrounds. For some, the tears started early. For others, they would come later, encouraged along perhaps by a post-match beer or two.

By lunchtime, the Kassam was filling up with fans, too. Soon, an entire side of the stadium – a stadium, it has to be said, with only three sides and a gaping hole where the fourth would typically stand – was packed. Packed with Mickey Lewis's old team-mates and fans, family and friends, all carrying with them their own memories of a man who'd impacted them profoundly. And it was an impressive roster at that. Chris Wilder. Des Buckingham. Jim Rosenthal. Steve McLaren. Jim Magilton.

Four different teams took to the pitch that afternoon. A pitch slick from the previous evening's rain, perfect for testing the goalkeeper from range or for a big tackle or two. Just as Mickey Lewis would have liked it. Oxford United were represented by two teams, including a fair number of their 2010 play-off final winners, wearing yellow shirts with Mickey's name printed in place of their famous bull logo. Oxford City were represented, too, in their distinctive blue-and-white hoops. A somewhat younger University of Oxford side rounded out the playing roster, in their customary dark blue.

The games were played hard. These were teams packed full of players who had played with or been coached by Mickey 'Mad Dog' Lewis, after all. Tackles flew in. Players argued with the referee. The lucky ones to find the net even celebrated their goals with a punch of the air and kiss of the badge. All whilst the stadium announcer soundtracked the action with reflections on memorable moments from Mickey's long and colourful playing and coaching career.

The biggest celebration of the day was reserved for the youngest player on the pitch. Making his Kassam debut, wearing a University of Oxford shirt with 'LEWIS 4' printed across the back, Mickey's eight-year-old son, Zach, sprinted on to the turf towards the end of the day's final match. Ten minutes later, he'd secured an accomplished hat-trick, a ride on the shoulders of an Oxford United legend or two and the acclaim of a stand full of fans on their feet, cheering and crying in equal measure.

No Mickey Lewis testimonial match would have been complete, of course, without a night in the bar and on the dancefloor. And so, it was over to Oxford City's Marsh Lane ground in nearby Marston for a hog roast, pork scratchings and a few keg-loads of Guinness. A feast that was followed exactly as Mickey would have designed it himself – with a karaoke rotation of Lionel Richie, Queen and Frank Sinatra.

No doubt as a sign of a good night of celebration – in that strange, bittersweet way memorials often have – several of the day's participants missed the last train back to London. And so it was that they returned home on a 3am bus, stumbling back home just as the sun broke on the following morning.

Looking back on the day – an emotionally charged, nostalgic and, at times, riotous day of football, beer and celebration – one of the dawn-treaders found a moment of clarity in the early morning haze: 'There was a bit of Mickey Lewis in that.'

* * *

It was only in the days and weeks that followed that we, the two authors of the book you now have in your hands, began to think a little more deeply on that particular piece of wisdom.

'There was a bit of Mickey Lewis in that.' Okay, sure. But what does that mean exactly?

Why were we all at the Kassam Stadium that day, in such numbers, for such a profoundly emotional afternoon? What exactly was it about Mickey Lewis that enabled him to have such an evidently outsized impact on those who watched him, those he played with, those who played and learned under him, and on his friends and his family?

The two of us – Leo Ackerman and Alex Urwin – played for him as captains of the University of Oxford first team. We understand how he shaped our approach to football, leadership and, ultimately, life. But what about all the other people in his life and at the Kassam Stadium on that day in late 2021? What did they think? What impact did Mickey have on them?

And so it was that we set out in search of an answer. Across the course of more or less a year, we've interviewed players, managers, commentators, fans, family members and friends. What we've found – the story of a remarkable player and coach and an even more remarkable man – is presented in the pages that follow.

* * *

We will soon start in the obvious place: Mickey's career as a professional footballer.

He played well over 400 times towards the top of the professional game. That is no mean feat and he certainly left his mark. To his team-mates, friends and fans, he was their 'Mad Dog'. And to those he played against? Well, one of the quotes on the back cover, somewhat spuriously attributed to Sir

Bobby Robson, suggests that players like Mickey were 'ruining the beautiful game one tackle at a time'.

But for those without allegiance to West Bromwich Albion, Derby County, Oxford United – or, at a stretch, Iowa's Des Moines Menace – Mickey's name might not register. The likes of Paul Gascoigne and Alan Shearer are more likely flag-bearers for 1980s and 1990s English football.

A first look at Mickey's coaching career tells a similar story. He certainly achieved a lot, in the esteemed surrounds of the dugout at Wembley and the more curious realities of one of the oldest rivalries in English football, the Varsity Match. But clearly neither of those achievements add up to the record of a Guardiola or even an Allardyce.

So, Mickey was not what you would consider a famous or glamorous footballer. Or indeed a famous or glamorous football manager or coach.

When we asked renowned broadcaster Jim Rosenthal to share some thoughts for the introduction to this book – as a man who knew Mickey well from their respective periods of time associated with Oxford United – he reflected that:

'People like Mickey Lewis don't usually have books written about them. Mickey was a proper pro with a fantastic attitude. But spending most of his career in the football trenches at unfashionable clubs? Who's interested in that? Where's the stardust? Where are the saucy headlines? Where's the glitz and glamour?'

But for anyone who was at the Kassam Stadium that day in October 2021, Mickey's is clearly a story that reaches beyond the boundaries of a generally successful playing and coaching career, spent for large parts in the football trenches that Rosenthal describes.

Rosenthal clearly agreed:

> 'His character, his zest for life, and his amazing ability to help and inspire players of all levels make his a story that demands to be told. His total commitment and devotion to the cause guaranteed that he surpassed the achievements of more naturally gifted players. If you could bottle that very special cocktail, every team would want some. And in the sometimes spiteful world of football, you would have to dig very deep to find anyone with a bad word to say about him, with the possible exception of those on the receiving end of one of his committed challenges.'

Indeed, almost without exception, everyone that spent time with Mickey knew him as Rosenthal describes here. So many of Mickey's fans, team-mates, friends and family told us that he was one of the most influential people in their lives.

That, we think, is a story worth telling.

So, in the pages, memories and anecdotes that follow, you will certainly meet a player whose bloody-minded will to win made him a cult hero at some of English football's historic clubs. A player many called a hero in that sepia-tinted era that preceded the false nines, low blocks and inverted full-backs of the Premier League.

We hope this book serves as something of a time capsule for a bygone era of English football, in addition to being a deeply researched biography of one of that era's most committed players.

Once the centre circle is traded for the dugout, you will certainly meet an extraordinary coach – and at times a manager – whose skill on the training ground was matched only by his ability to inspire off it.

Most of all, though, you will find a story that is bigger than any of its component parts.

Indeed, we hope you will be moved by the story of a man whose outsized impact on so many people continues to last far beyond his short battle with cancer, which tragically ended in early 2021, with Mickey aged just 56.

* * *

Now before we begin in earnest, there is some housekeeping to attend to.

There is some controversy over the spelling of Mickey's name. In the course of our research, we found team sheets and programmes, including the programme from Mickey's memorial game, that used the spelling 'Micky'.

One Oxford local journalist insisted that Mickey himself had corroborated that spelling, but he'd just never thought it important enough to correct all the errors over the years.

Those who knew Mickey will appreciate that the local journalist's story is certainly plausible. But you'll have noticed from the cover and this introduction that we'll be using 'Mickey'. We've been told that when Mickey set up his email address, he did it with an 'e', because that was how he wanted it. So, naturally, that's good enough for us.

We also wanted to note here that this book is not a straightforwardly chronological account of Mickey's life as a player and then coach. Whilst we do begin by chronicling Mickey's career, we wanted this story to be enjoyed without requiring an Oxford United season ticket as the price of entry. That's especially the case given neither of us count any of Mickey's professional clubs as our own. And neither of us are football archivists, historians or statisticians.

What follows instead is a story structured according to the adages by which Mickey lived, led and left a mark on so many of those he encountered.

The first section, 'Guaranteeing A Performance', which is split into two parts, tells the story of Mickey's development as a player and then as a coach and sometime manager. Across both parts, it's a story of a man who gave everything to football and demanded all those around him do the same. And in the second part, we spend time diving into one of Mickey's favourite days in football: Oxford United's Conference play-off final win at Wembley in 2010.

'Don't Let It Pass You By' then charts Mickey's unique skill for coaching young players, thus exploring the impact he had on thousands of young lives, including our own.

From there, 'enjoy the occasion' goes on to reflect on Mickey as a man who took seriously the need and obligation to enjoy the ride, and all of life's ups and downs, particularly once the final whistle had been blown.

And the book then finishes as Mickey would have insisted when a team-mate motioned to leave the pub at 10pm, with 'One for the Road'.

* * *

There are just a couple more things to add here. Whilst we were both lucky enough to play for Mickey during his time coaching the University of Oxford's first team, this story is not ours. This story belongs to all who played with, played against, watched, were coached by or simply knew of Mickey Lewis.

So *Mad Dog* would not have been possible without the remarkable generosity of the hundred-plus contributors who gave us their time and their memories from every stage of Mickey's life.

There is a full list of those contributors set out at the end of the book. But we want to say thank you here to a few people who went above and beyond to help us write this book. Jim Rosenthal gave us his time and the comments that guided the introduction. And it was a thrill and privilege to speak with some of the players, managers and commentators whom we grew up watching and listening to as we both developed our own lifelong love of football; thanks, in particular, to Ron Atkinson, Martin Tyler, Peter Drury, Chris Wilder, Jim Magilton and Mark Lawrenson.

And, of course, this book simply wouldn't have been possible without Suzanne Lewis, who introduced us to almost every person we interviewed and who kept us on the straight and narrow throughout. We also want to thank Suzanne for choosing See Saw, the charity to which we'll be donating any proceeds from this project.

With that, and noting of course that any and all errors that follow are completely ours, we hope you enjoy reading Mickey's story as much as we've enjoyed telling it.

And if nothing else, Zach, this book is for you.

SECTION ONE PART I:

GUARANTEEING A PERFORMANCE

Chapter One

You can't guarantee a result, but …

'You can't guarantee a result. But you can absolutely guarantee a performance.'

Mickey Lewis, in dressing rooms and on touchlines
across the country, from the 1970s through to 2021

'Mickey Lewis would tackle anything that moved.'

Brian Horton, Oxford United manager, early 1990s

WHAT FOLLOWS in the first section of this book is the story of a scruffy, bushy-haired boy from Birmingham and how he became a beloved 'Mad Dog' in one of English football's defining eras and then a beloved and highly respected coach.

It's a story that jumps from the Midlands to the suburbs of Cannes. From The Hawthorns to Wembley. From Des Moines, Iowa, to the University of Oxford. And through all the centre circles and touchlines along the way.

And it's a story that, ultimately, celebrates a man who inspired hundreds if not thousands of fans, team-mates, colleagues and players he coached by how he played, how he taught the game and how he lived. Knowing above all that whilst you can never guarantee a result, you can always, always guarantee a performance.

* * *

We start as the late 1970s edge into the 1980s. Back when Rod Stewart could dominate the charts. When Wembley still had two towers. When Sir Alex Ferguson was still a glint in Manchester United's eye.

As for the football itself? Well, neither of us were there. Of course, we've seen *The Football Factory*. But, really, we're 20-something Ipswich Town and Tottenham Hotspur fans who grew up long after European glory had been and gone at Portman Road and during a time in which the most exciting things happening at White Hart Lane were American football matches and Lady Gaga concerts. A far cry from the days of Sir Bobby Robson, Ossie Ardiles or Glenn Hoddle.

So, we thought it useful to do some asking around.

Now, who exactly to ask?

Fans in England watch a lot of football. From the pre-match chip shop dwellers of the Tottenham High Road to the Suffolk ale drinkers on Portman Road, they know all there is to know. Or so they'd like to think, at least.

Season ticket holders immerse themselves in the particular sights, sounds and smells of the beautiful game for 38 or 46 games a season. The lucky ones even get a cup run or two. Every Saturday or Tuesday is a new milestone around which years and lives are shaped and measured. A new opportunity for a defining hero or a villain. For a plot twist or a cliffhanger ending.

The managers are experts, too, of course. Not quite like the fans. They certainly don't walk down the high street and hear the pre-match chatter or see the misplaced hope in the eyes of a young child on the bus. But they get the front row seat. The privileged spot from which to think about the next problem, the next solution, the next big moment in a game, a season, a career.

But there's one group of people that we think stand out from all the rest: the commentators. They're the perfect hybrid of fan and manager. Of passion and analysis. Of heart and of head.

They see games like the fans. They even sit amongst the fans, with the gantries – the booths from which the commentators work – often planted on top of or next to a packed home stand. At Everton's Goodison Park, one has to walk through rows 16 and 17 of the Bullens Road to get to the commentary seating. And sometimes the commentators behave like fans, too; Gary Neville can't resist a groan when Manchester United concede.

Yet they get all the access and insight to the game's premier coaches and tacticians, walking freely in the corridors and beside the pitches of the country's most famous footballing theatres, week in, week out.

And no one – living, at least – stands out from the rest quite like Martin Tyler.

From the 1978 World Cup to the 2023 FA Cup Final, from the gantry at The Den to the VIP deck in Doha, he has seen the game at its best and at its worst, with a healthy dose of everything in between.

And as Mickey Lewis signed his first professional contract at West Bromwich Albion in 1981, aged 16 and a product of the Baggies' academy, Tyler was in the process of being selected to lead the ITV team at the 1982 World Cup in Spain.

So, who better to start off with than him? Who better to introduce us to the world and era in which Mickey's story exists?

Tyler's foremost reflection of that time?

'I get annoyed when people say there was nothing before the Premier League. On the pitch, the game hasn't changed much. It's always been the first whistle to last, always tribal in its nature. The desire to win was just as strong.'

As Tyler continued, it was clear that, in many respects, English football as the late 1970s turned to the early 1980s was the same competitive, romantic, unpredictable beast we know and love today. There were the same unlikely title charges and cup upsets. The same conversations and concerns amongst the fans. The same possibility that, for 90 minutes or a season, life can mean something a little bigger, a little more.

We found one programme during the course of our research – from a match between Oxford United and Leicester City from the era in which Mickey was playing – that included a piece from Mark Shanahan on the growing competition between broadcasters to cover the sport. 'It wouldn't surprise me if Sky wins,' he writes, rather presciently, considering that the network currently broadcasts the majority of the Premier League games shown live in the UK each season. The same programme includes a price list for Oxford United's merchandise. Fifty pounds for a large adult shell suit seems a little expensive.

So, maybe Tyler was right. Much was similar.

Of course, that's not to say it was *exactly* the same.

There was no VAR, no 80 per cent possession or inverted full-backs, no underlapping centre-halves. There certainly weren't the red cards there are today for tackles that once raised neither an eyebrow nor a fist. And there was no social media or content overload; when a teenaged Mickey signed that first professional contract at 16, West Brom had only just hired their first photographer and his photos weren't available until a week after the game.

Anton Rogan, one of Mickey's Oxford United team-mates and an eventual Celtic stalwart, is somewhat nostalgic about the relationship between players and match officials back when he and Mickey were starting out. 'You could actually talk to refs and linesmen as human beings. If you told them to fuck off, they'd tell you to fuck off back and that was it.'

And the stadiums and the pitches were not quite as glamorous as we've come to know in the Premier League era. Tyler recalls having to lie down for most of the game when Oxford hosted Portsmouth at what he described, perhaps a little euphemistically, as the 'homely and friendly' Manor Ground early in his commentary career.

So, with that context set – with all the similarities and differences to today's game established – our story can begin.

Chapter Two

'The Europeans didn't love getting kicked around by him'

*'I remember playing in a youth game against
Mickey when he was at West Brom. I was a winger
and, in the changing room before the game, our
manager told me to watch out for Mickey Lewis.
I'd never seen him or heard of him before. But after
a few minutes, I'd seen him, I'd heard of him and
I'd felt him. For the rest of the game, I stayed as far
away from him as I could.'*

Martin Allen, West Ham United midfielder and
experienced English football manager

WITHOUT REACHING for too much amateur psychology,
understanding a young Mickey – who would quickly establish
himself as a combative 'Mad Dog' on the pitch and a gentleman
off it – requires an understanding of the nature and nurture of
his childhood.

As a young boy and then teenager, Mickey had a
straightforward, loving upbringing in the Midlands. It was a life

much like that of a lot of young boys his age. Except, that is, for one thing. He had a prodigious talent for football – standing out amongst his peers almost immediately – and as soon as he was old enough to realise this fact, he could think of little else that he wanted to do with his life. He wanted to be a professional footballer, ideally for his beloved Birmingham City.

In the end, it was West Brom who took a chance, picking up Mickey from one of the area's local amateur leagues. In joining the Baggies, Mickey was linking up with his firm friend Peter Frain, who lived nearby in Acocks Green.

'I was so delighted when Mickey got picked up by Albion,' Frain recalled. '[He] wasn't the most flamboyant of players, but he had this determination, this attitude, a lot more than mine.'

Of course, a dream stays exactly that, a dream, without a remarkable dose of application and resilience. And these were qualities instilled in Mickey from a young age. As several people, including Frain, who knew them put it, 'his parents were just good people'. And that was borne out in their commitment to ensuring Mickey had every opportunity to progress as he moved through the West Brom academy, as well as the deep appreciation of hard work he would need to seize them.

Mickey's father worked for the Royal Mail and was Mickey's chauffeur, as well as one of his foremost role models. Such was his generosity, Mickey wasn't the only one to benefit. One of Mickey's academy team-mates didn't have a car in the family and so several times a week he'd be round at Mickey's house, waiting outside for Mickey to burst through the front door, his dad strolling behind, ready for another Midlands football adventure. 'God bless his dad,' another of Mickey's academy friends from the time said. 'Forty-five-minute journeys, sometimes two hours, just with the radio on and chirpy lads talking rubbish in the back.'

That commitment, from Mickey, but also from his family, was soon rewarded. Mickey would make his first-team debut for West Brom the same year he signed his first professional contract, aged just 16.

Before that debut, though, Mickey also enjoyed significant recognition as a youth player, including for England.

* * *

The Stade Pierre de Coubertin in Cannes is the 10,000-seater home to a club, AS Cannes, that does not appear to have produced any footballers of any great note. Unless you count Sébastien Amoros, a Cannes local who made ten appearances for Port Vale in 2016.

Amoros aside, the most notable piece of AS Cannes history seems to be the fact that, in the 2014/15 season, they were banned from French football for financial mismanagement.

Beyond that, the Coubertin is not a particularly famous football stadium. It's not even the main attraction in a ritzy Cote d'Azur town better known for its glamorous film festival. It doesn't have a nickname. Nor does it sound like it deserves one.

But, despite all this, the Coubertin was, through the middle of the last century, the regular host stadium for the Tournois Junior, a yearly youth tournament with a history that evokes a different world, both in terms of the politics and the football.

The 1957 Tournois final saw the young men of AS Cannes and Fiorentina share a goalless draw, with the match report doing little more than noting that they won five corners apiece. The home side were declared the winners on average squad age, which in a youth tournament must have been a close-run thing.

In 1973, it was not just club sides enjoying competitive football in the French sun. The mighty Argentina competed and made the final. A final in which they played and scraped past Leeds United, drawing 1-1 but ultimately winning 7-3 – on corners.

In 1978, the Soviet Union beat Iran by one goal to nil and the Netherlands won their group after drawing lots. Two years later, East Germany lost the seventh-place play-off versus Spain.

So, a different world, indeed.

The tournament was still going strong by the summer of 1982 and at 17, a year after signing his first professional contract with West Brom and having already made a handful of appearances for the club's first team, Mickey was invited to join the illustrious list of young footballers that had graced the prestigious tournament. He would be representing England's age group side, alongside friend and Baggies team-mate Frain.

The pair's journey to Cannes would be unrecognisable to the modern, monied footballer, relying as it did on a combination of planes, trains and automobiles, and parents taking time off work to facilitate parts of the journey.

Arriving at a similar tournament today would surely involve a private transfer, Italian leather seats and washbags, and a mandatory Instagram post for at least a few thousand followers. César Palacios, a zippy Real Madrid Castilla striker, arrived at the 2023 UEFA Under-19 Championship in a brand new, gifted pair of adidas trainers, family in tow, all paid for and wearing the same top-of-the-range shoes. If he continues to bang in the goals, Palacios could feasibly earn tens of millions in La Liga. Not a financial future Mickey, Frain or any of their England youth team-mates would have been expecting.

But unglamorous journey or not, Mickey arrived in Cannes with a spring in his step, a mark to make and some similarly young and ambitious international footballers on which to make it.

In a frightening schedule that would have the modern mega managers and club lawyers writing strongly worded letters to the first football administrator they could find, Mickey's England side played four games in six days against Portugal, Netherlands, Czechoslovakia and France. The physiotherapists on the tour – if there were any – and the Stade Pierre de Coubertin's groundstaff must have worked round the clock. Mickey, whose knees would later pay the price, played in every game.

Two comfortable wins were followed by two close-fought 1-0 losses, the second in the final to France. Plus ça change.

Frain, who came on for Mickey halfway through the final against the French, remembers the integral role Mickey played throughout the tournament: 'Mickey was the centre pin, the engine and he was very, very aggressive.' Unsurprisingly, Frain notes that 'the Europeans didn't love getting kicked around by him'.

Despite that disappointment against France, the group did triumph at a follow-up tournament in Yugoslavia the year after Cannes.

But neither Mickey nor any of his team-mates from those two tournaments ultimately graduated to become full England internationals. In all likelihood, they were not considered a vintage group, given the team in the year that followed their Cannes outing boasted Martin Keown and Tony Adams, with a certain Teddy Sheringham getting some time from the bench.

But the world of professional men's football was ahead of Mickey. The game was there to be played. And whilst he knew he couldn't guarantee the result – no one can – he was already demonstrating that he'd be sure as anything to guarantee a performance.

Chapter Three

Becoming Mad Dog

MUCH IS made in football about the importance of the first tackle.

Neil 'Razor' Ruddock, Vinnie Jones and just about every Sunday league coach in the country have said something along the lines of: 'Let 'em know you're there early doors. Win that first challenge and they won't wanna come back for a second.'

Does it actually make a difference? The sports science departments of major clubs can probably now show you a detailed statistical study on how the first tackle has zero impact on goals scored, goals conceded or the percentage chance of winning.

Then again, maybe it's one of those unquantifiable but undeniably useful acts in football, like staying after the game to sign autographs for young fans.

And the first tackle of the first professional match of your career? We'd like to think that's got to count for something, quantifiable or not.

Like he would go on to do for the next two decades – decades he would spend building a career towards the top of the English game – Mickey made that first tackle count.

The setting was a tie in the fourth round of the League Cup – England's second-most prestigious cup competition – at Selhurst Park on a bitterly cold December evening in 1981, a matter of months after Mickey had signed his first professional contract.

Playing at the time in the second tier of English football, Crystal Palace were the side hosting a top-flight West Bromwich Albion team whose glory days were fast slipping away.

Managed by 'Big' Ron Atkinson, Albion had recently reached the latter stages of the UEFA Cup – Europe's second-most prestigious cup competition – and recorded their highest league position in 20 years, finishing third in the top tier. They'd been breaking ground, too, having fielded three black players in the 1978 season – Cyrille Regis, Laurie Cunningham and Brendon Batson – the first time a club of such stature had ever regularly done so.

By 1981, however, Atkinson took the impossible-to-turn-down Manchester United job and club talisman Bryan Robson soon went to join him.

Having just about recovered from an early 1970s relegation and record low attendances, Albion fans were suddenly facing another period of decline.

But, of course, there are moments and people that can delight and soothe a pained fanbase. Even if those fans know that their team's great future is now behind them.

In the 75th minute of the cup tie against Palace, with Albion already 2-1 up, Mickey's entrance did just that.

He had already made his mark on the squad. The Albion photographer at the time, Laurence Rampling, recalls that: 'Every player in the first team at the club looked at Mickey and thought "Wow, this boy is *good*. He had this tenacity about him, he had this confidence about him."' Mark Grew, who played at Albion from 1976 to 1983, told us that Mickey already 'had a reputation for not backing out of any tackle, well before he made the transition up from the youth squad'.

It was a reputation he had established when stepping up and training with the first team. As Martin Jol put it:

'Mickey was playing in a five-a-side with us, and it looked like this had been going on for years. I had never seen a kid playing like him, playing like an old professional, strong like a beast and tenacious like Nobby Stiles in his prime.

'He looked like a captain already. A leader in the making, with one ambition: showing everybody that he was ready to play. He had been taught to keep it simple and never lose it, but if you lose it, get it back in seconds. Good advice, but for me, perhaps even a bit too simple, because the boy could play.'

And whilst he might have been on the small side, even for a youth player, he'd fast taken to heart a particular piece of advice dispensed to him by former Albion player-manager Johnny

Giles, the man responsible for one of the most successful periods in Albion's history: 'When you're a little one, you gotta make sure they feel ya.'

But training ground reputation and Johnny Giles wisdom aside, he was still relatively unknown to all but the most devoted of the Albion fanbase and that breed of fan that makes it their business to track the developments of their club's academy system.

So, when the substitution was announced, the travelling fans, tucked away in the corner of Selhurst Park and likely still pining for Robson, craned their necks to see who exactly it was coming on to the pitch to help their side see out the match. While they might have missed the announcement of the name whilst singing for star striker Cyrille Regis, or indeed not recognised the name at all, they couldn't miss the diminutive, frizzy-haired youngster who was soon bounding on to the turf.

'He was all frizzy and all curly! And friendly. And bolshie.' So chuckled Rampling.

'Bolshie' Mickey and his curls began his professional debut, strong thighs showing beneath five-inch shorts and socks pulled up over the knees. At 16 years and 303 days, he was at the time Albion's third-youngest first-team player and the youngest player ever to appear in the League Cup.

Now, it's hard to know exactly what was going through Mickey's head as he stood there in the centre circle, surveying his new home: the professional game. But there's a fair chance he was recalling that advice from Johnny Giles. 'Make sure they feel ya.' Or, as a variation on the theme, that old favourite: 'Let 'em know you're there early doors.'

Is it still early doors if it's the 75th minute? Early doors in a career, perhaps.

A loose ball bounced away from a Crystal Palace central midfielder. The kind of loose ball that West Brom, Derby County and Oxford United fans would soon come to know as a prelude to one thing: a Mickey Lewis tackle.

Mickey's eyes likely lit up. His heels certainly left the grass. The away fans, craving one of the thunderous challenges seemingly reserved for the latter stages of a cup tie, sat slightly out of their seats.

It was a 50-50 challenge soon to become a 99-1. Both men charged towards the ball. The younger of the two was desperate to make his mark.

'Make sure they feel ya.'

'Let 'em know you're there early doors.'

The ball squirmed away. The Palace midfielder went with it as Mickey slid through him and another few metres of clipped grass. Whether or not it had touched Mickey's boot was a minor detail. The desired effect had been achieved. The opposite man knew he was there. The West Brom fans, now roaring their side into the final minutes, did too.

Of course, so too did the referee. Mickey was booked just a few seconds later. Two minutes after coming on for his professional debut. It was one of the fastest ever debutant bookings in the history of English football. It also wouldn't be the last time he was booked on a debut.

But it was the 1980s. This was English football. And that was Mickey.

The 'bolshie' Brummie had made his mark on the shinpads of the unsuspecting Crystal Palace midfielder – just as he had done when training up with the first team – and now he had his sights set on anyone else who'd dare compete with him for a loose ball in the middle of the park.

It was the full-blooded approach – the guarantee a performance approach – that would, before long earn him his 'Mad Dog' nickname.

And it was an approach that would soon reveal itself to be the defining quality of both his professional and personal life.

Chapter Four

'Plays like a frisky puppy'

MICKEY WAS soon making a name for himself at West Brom, picking up appearances in the first team – which remained in England's top division – and establishing himself as someone who could do an effective defensive job for his manager.

And it wasn't long before he was making his full home debut against Brian Clough's recently all-conquering Nottingham Forest, just before his 17th birthday, in February 1982.

A matter of months after his memorable appearance from the bench against Crystal Palace, he was told 24 hours before kick-off that he'd be starting. In an Oxford United programme interview many years later, far from remembering a moment of intense nervousness or doubt, as it might be fair to expect, Mickey described the occasion as the most memorable game of his career. A day on which injuries created an opportunity, a day on which he was thrown in and a day on which his Birmingham-based family had assembled en masse to support him.

And from that Nottingham Forest game, which West Brom won 2-1 and in which Mickey returned a mature performance in the centre of midfield – with one report noting 'a curly-headed youngster demonstrated that he could provide the aggression needed to add steel to the undoubted finesse in midfield' – he set about trying to pick up as many first-team appearances as he could.

The starts didn't come rapidly. He was a teenager and West Brom were playing in the First Division, England's top tier. But by September 1983, with Mickey still just 18, he was entrusted with a clear task for what would be his ninth appearance for the first team, against West Ham. As he put it himself for a piece of pre-match reporting: 'I've been told to keep an eye on Trevor Brooking.'

Now, by the time of his encounter with Mickey, long-time England international Brooking was coming to the end of his West Ham career. His last cap for the national team had come the year before at the World Cup finals. But he was still one of the English game's most notable stars.

For many, it would have been an intimidating task. But Mickey was already proving himself to be an unusually mature competitor: 'I admire Brooking enormously but I'm not his sort of player. I'm more of a Billy Bremner. I'm looking forward to the game more than any other I've played.'

West Brom won the game 1-0 and as far as the post-match reporting was concerned, Mickey had more than risen to the challenge. West Brom's much-loved statman, John Homer, remembered that Mickey 'marked Brooking right out of the game'. One journalist suggested that Mickey 'submerged West Ham's experienced Trevor Brooking, football's number one gentleman'. So much so, in fact, that Brooking was apparently 'visibly ruffled by some of [Mickey's] tackling'. It would not be the last time that one of the country's most gifted players felt that way after a 90-minute midfield bout with Mickey as their combative opposite number. That comparison to Billy Bremner, Leeds United's 'ten stone of barbed wire', was already proving an astute one.

And so it was that fan favourite and club legend Cyrille Regis was soon describing Mickey as 'a great asset to our side' and someone he 'would have in my team any time'. From a player like Regis, who was awarded an MBE for his services to football and was honoured with a statue outside West Brom's Hawthorns stadium, that's high praise indeed. Others agreed. One journalist wrote not long after that West Ham match that Albion had a 'star of international quality in their possession'.

In advance of a Milk Cup match against local rivals Aston Villa a couple of months later, in November 1983, one local newspaper singled out Mickey as a rare cause for hope for Albion's suffering supporters after another defeat and a continuation of a dismal run of form:

> 'In the days when 60,000 cloth caps rocked up, 22 players cared passionately at £20 per week. On Saturday, there was hardly an Albion player who deserved that amount, though most of them are paid more than a multiple of 20. There is no reason mercenaries – except for self-respect and a duty to paying customers – should bother about ancient tribal rivalries.

'But those Albion players who strolled through the first hour of football, posing with outside-of-the-foot passes, pretending to go for 50-50 balls and portraying themselves as dedicated followers of football fashion should be told that their first-team services are not required next Wednesday or in the foreseeable future.

'Oh, for a trier like Mickey Lewis!'

And it wasn't just players like Regis or that journalist developing a fondness for Mickey. As the Lewis family scrapbooks show, it was around this time that he started receiving his first fan mail. One young female fan, who we'll call Kay, spoke at length of her support for West Brom, before finishing her letter bluntly: 'I think you are very nice.'

Perhaps writing together for courage, Estelle and Karen mused that Mickey might well have received their letters (plural) and thought 'Oh God, it's those mad teenage girls again, what do they want this time?' Reading the letter in question, it seems they wanted more correspondence and more signed photographs, given such trophies had been causing 'quite the stir' at school.

It's a great shame that none of Mickey's replies made it to the family archives.

* * *

In November 1984, a year after that Milk Cup match against Aston Villa, Mickey was 19 and he boasted an impressive 33 games in the Albion midfield. He had won the club's young player of the year award. And he still had two years on his contract.

But this would be the extent of his involvement for the Baggies. He was sold to Derby County, who had just been relegated to England's third tier. The fee would be just shy of £30,000.

Albion manager Johnny Giles – who incidentally was already Mickey's fourth manager in his relatively brief stint in the professional game – was quick to stress that the move was no insult to Mickey's ability. It was simply an opportunity, so Giles put it, for him to get the regular football he needed at such a formative stage in his career.

In an introductory interview for the Derby fans, Mickey himself suggested that he hadn't wanted to leave the club that had given him his chance in the professional game, but it had been necessary to 'fulfil [himself]'.

None of the above stopped Martin Jol reacting with disbelief. Reflecting now on the transfer, he said: 'Believe you me, I was sure that Mickey Lewis was good enough to play for his beloved Baggies throughout the next decade.'

Regardless, although Mickey's surroundings may have changed and while he suddenly found himself further from the top of the game than people like Jol ever expected him to be, his footballing philosophy remained as consistent as ever. It was still very much the case for Mickey that to play the game well was to play it hard and, at the very minimum, to guarantee a performance.

He got booked on his debut, just like at West Brom. His playing style was soon being described in the local press as that of a 'frisky puppy'. And as the Derby fansite *dcfcfans.uk* describes that first season – in which Mickey played ten matches and earned a new contract – the consistency of the reporting compared with his time at West Brom is remarkable.

'One of the toughest players to ever pull on a Rams shirt.' 'The best player at the club when the opposition had the ball.' And perhaps the best of the lot: 'I remember him absolutely smashing Steve McMahon.' To which another fan replied: 'I remember that well, too, but not as well as McMahon. He was a passenger for the rest of the game, probably looking over his shoulder wondering where Mickey was.'

The fact Mickey is remembered primarily for a tackle might suggest an otherwise underwhelming period in Derby colours. But watching the highlights of the match in question – against Liverpool in 1988 – it soon becomes clear exactly why 23-year-old Mickey's performance that afternoon is now so well secured in the club's folklore.

The match itself had some significance, though only really for Liverpool. Kenny Dalglish's team needed to avoid defeat against a Derby side that included England's renowned goalkeeper Peter Shilton to equal the Leeds United record of 29 matches unbeaten from the start of a First Division season. A 1-1 draw in front of 26,000 fans did the job for a side packed full of talent: Bruce Grobbelaar, Alan Hansen, Peter Beardsley, John Barnes. But, thanks in no small part to Mickey, they didn't leave the match completely unscathed.

John Motson is the commentator, his voice dipping in and out of the still-available highlights video. He describes the tackle on McMahon – which is thunderous and very clearly illegal – in amusingly understated fashion, perhaps reflective of a long-passed threshold for foul play: 'McMahon goes down rather awkwardly and clearly in some pain.'

Such a tackle would surely elicit far greater outrage today and likely even a video-assisted red card if the referee hadn't got there first. Either way, it's clear from the tackle that Mickey's approach to his first outing for West Brom against Crystal Palace was not out of character, nor the afternoon Mickey spent in close quarters with Trevor Brooking.

When watching the highlights in full, it becomes clear, remarkably, that the tackle on McMahon wasn't actually Mickey's most full-blooded involvement during that match at Derby's Baseball Ground, despite the memories of those posters on *dcfcfans.uk*.

Midway through the first half, the ball bounces towards John Barnes in the centre circle. A rare poor touch costs him. There is Mickey, never far away, thundering in and through Barnes. At first sight, the tackle looks painful. On a modern, slowed-down replay, it would surely have looked criminal. Indeed, everything Barnes went on to achieve suddenly seems miraculous having watched this particular encounter, in which Mickey's right boot practically bends his tibia backwards.

For what might have been the first time in his career, Motson was momentarily speechless.

'This lad in the middle there, Mickey Lewis, has a reputation for being one of the most, well, uh, I was going to say competitive players in the league. That was a bit more than competitive.'

Between those two tackles on McMahon and Barnes, anyone at the Baseball Ground on that day in 1988 will have left in no doubt as to exactly how the 'Mad Dog' acquired, and lived up to, his name.

'He's certainly a ball-winner is Lewis,' said Motson.

He certainly was.

Chapter Five

'Quite clearly he wasn't Trevor Hebberd'

'With several crunching tackles, one over-the-top challenge which brought him a booking, a rash swing of the leg on the edge of the area which gave away a penalty and a remarkable display of non-stop running and commitment, it was just another day at the office for [Mickey Lewis]'

An extract from an article in the *Oxford Mail*

DESPITE A string of memorable moments in the Derby midfield – typically involving a more technically gifted opposition player – Mickey never quite cemented his place in the team.

He was still receiving a healthy stream of incoming fan mail. As those same Lewis family scrapbooks show, someone who we'll call Louise wrote to him towards the end of his time at the club to thank him for all his efforts at the Baseball Ground. 'What an asset it is,' she said, 'to have somebody in this day and age actually enjoy what they're doing and believe in themselves.'

But having been in and out of the side as Derby secured promotion back into England's second tier in the 1985/86 season, he didn't feature at all the following year as Derby secured a double bounce straight into the First Division. And in that top tier, despite appearances against Arsenal and Manchester United, he certainly wasn't a regular starter.

Those family newspaper clippings give a sense as to why that was the case. Derby manager Arthur Cox was as complimentary as everyone else about Mickey's ball-winning ability. But he lamented his tendency to 'pass the ball with the same speed that he has won it'. Cox added that 'he has been in too much of a rush and that makes him look as if all he can do is tackle people'.

And so it was that Mickey was spending his early 20s playing for the club's reserves in what was then called the Central League, now replaced by the far more comfortable world of under-23s football. As Mickey himself put it at the time: 'I was beginning to wonder where I stood. The gaffer always told me that I was part of the squad but I felt I was beginning to get a bit bogged down.'

So, while Derby had awarded Mickey an extended contract at the end of his first season with the club, it should perhaps be no surprise that 50 games and one goal later, at the age of 23, Mickey moved on. He left the Baseball Ground late in the summer of 1988. And in a deal that saw the accomplished midfielder Trevor Hebberd go the other way, he headed south for the first time in his life and career, to Oxford United.

It was a move in which Mickey jumped between two clubs owned by the infamous Robert Maxwell, the highly controversial press baron and father of Ghislaine Maxwell, who would later become a convicted sex offender. And just as he had done when moving from West Brom to Derby, Mickey was joining a newly relegated club. Oxford had just slipped out of the top tier and would play the 1988/89 season in the Second Division.

Mickey would eventually go on to achieve cult hero status at Oxford, making 350 appearances in the United midfield. That can make it easy to forget he was replacing a fan favourite in Hebberd. A fan favourite who had scored the opening goal in United's famous League Cup victory in 1986. So, despite the progress Mickey had made in the game since his professional debut, he still faced a real challenge to get the fans on board.

Oxford Radio's Jerome Sale remembers Mickey's signing: 'The fans were very sad to see Hebberd go. He was a Rolls-Royce of a player and Mickey wasn't. The fans, actually, were quite unsure about him.'

From his vantage point as a long-time member of the media team at Oxford United and now general manager at nearby non-league side Oxford City, Chris Williams was a little more blunt.

'Quite clearly, he wasn't Trevor Hebberd. He just wasn't in the physical shape that Trevor was. I remember Oxford United's manager saying that he needed to cut out the Mars bars. He was, shall we say, chunky. He wasn't able to get around the pitch like Trevor.'

So, Mickey arrived in Oxford a bit overweight, a little too slow and in shoes many seemed to think were too big to fill. A tough ask. Or a tough ask for other, less confident or committed operators.

Even as Mickey was asked to play at centre-half in the early stages of his Oxford career and whilst he was conscious of the comparisons to Hebberd – which he felt unfair given they were such different players – Mickey worked desperately to win over the fans and he knew exactly how to do so. He always had done.

'He started to kick people up in the air,' says Williams. And as Williams continued:

> 'He really won fans over. He wasn't big enough, but he'd go in for challenges and win them. They loved the passion. They loved the aggression. They loved the way that he played. He was a holding midfielder, but it was other people he was holding.
>
> 'He had this peculiar way of putting his arms out to the side, making it harder to get round him, like a little hairy roundabout. And if you got round him, he'd kick you.'

In a beautiful ode to the straightforward pleasures of the English football fan, it really was as simple as that.

* * *

So it was that Mickey was soon establishing himself as a regular in the Oxford United side in a period that first saw them grounded in the middle-to-lower reaches of the Second Division table, before the league was redesignated formally as Division One upon the First Division's conversion to the Premier League in 1992.

Oxford would move between Division One and Division Two throughout the 1990s and the remainder of Mickey's time as a player. But if Oxford's fortunes were not always upward bound, the reports from that period of Mickey's career were overwhelmingly positive. After he'd shed half a stone on manager Brian Horton's instructions, he was soon earning regular plaudits.

The local press from the time is particularly instructive. 'Super Lewis crowned an all-action display with his first goal for Oxford.' And shortly after that first goal, one local newspaper column, by the curiously and surely falsely named Dick Tugwell, celebrated the importance of Oxford's 'defensive midfield terrier, the pro's professional, whose bite in the tackle is invariably more ferocious than his bark'. There was that Billy Bremner comparison again, at least indirectly.

Then, shortly after that, the best of the lot: a report heralding an all-action performance from 'Lewis the Lungs'. The game in question was a 2-2 draw between Oxford United and Mickey's former employers Derby County, back at the Baseball Ground in 1992. According to the report, Mickey, by this point 27, sprinted 70 yards to stab home Oxford's second, denting Derby's promotion hopes in the process. It was this act that earned him his aerobically themed nickname.

But even better still is Mickey's post-match interview:

'I wouldn't have been able to [make the 70-yard run] if I hadn't taken the advice of Arsenal manager George Graham. I read where he said footballers needed as much rest as possible. That was good enough for me.

'So, the only thing I do now after training is NOTHING! All day, every day, I just lie on the settee watching TV soaps all afternoon. I do make the wife's tea when she has finished work, but that's it.'

Judging by the stories of Mickey's off-pitch exploits, he is probably overstating exactly how rigorously he followed Graham's advice. But that's for later.

Chapter Six

'He could really play,' that Mickey Lewis

'He was always labelled Mad Dog. But, for me,
he was a lot better than that. He could really
play. He was a talented footballer. You'd always
want him on your team.'

Oxford United, Celtic and Northern Ireland
footballer Anton Rogan

AS A young West Brom player, Mickey once protested that whilst he '[could not] change [his] style of play', he was 'not a dirty player'. But we recognise that we haven't done much so far to support this contestation or, in fact, suggest he could play.

So, even whilst acknowledging the scepticism expressed as to Mickey's suitability for the tighter rules of the modern game, it's probably the right moment to set the record straight a little, as Mickey did himself in the process of building a successful career at Oxford United.

Yes, a web search for 'Mickey Lewis' doesn't return many videos of outside-of-the-boot passes or pinpoint crosses. Yes, you're more likely to find videos of bone-crunching tackles and interviews with former team-mates telling you how they'd wear shin pads at training when Mickey was there. Yes, he tackled hard. He kicked everything. For the *Oxford Mail*'s Mark Edwards, he was a 'real menace in the middle'.

But he was certainly more than that, too. All those who talked to us about Mickey's playing style and his 'Mad Dog' moniker, which really took hold in earnest after his move from Derby to Oxford, were quick to note they weren't dismissing him as a bruiser. 'He wasn't dirty' and 'I can't really remember him getting into trouble' were familiar refrains. Referees might well have rolled their eyes at the sight of Mickey on their pitch, but he was always careful to stay on the right side of them and be the first to shake their hands at the end of the game.

And one fan forum poster – using the pseudonym 'Scotch Egg' – recalled fondly that, whilst a chant of 'Mad Dog's gonna get ya' would often ring around the Manor Ground, they'd 'never seen such a hard player try to dominate games without hurting someone; there was never any malice, just 110 per cent commitment to the cause'.

So, whilst we don't want to overstate the extent to which Mickey was the 1980s or 1990s equivalent to the modern-day Rolls-Royce midfielder – the £100m deep-lying ball-winner-cum-playmaker to which Jim Rosenthal jokingly drew a comparison – we also don't want to reduce him to a caricature.

When looking back on Mickey's Oxford career in its entirety, it's important to balance talk of his combative playing style with an acknowledgement that, through his 20s – and through the early 1990s – he was no lower-league brute. In fact, he matured into an accomplished, top-level midfielder.

* * *

Like many of the midfield marshals and imperious centre-halves who go down in the collective fan consciousness as brutish and unsophisticated, Mickey's reputation sometimes clouded fans' ability to see some of his other qualities. But you simply don't clock up 400 games in centre midfield towards the top of English football without a number of strings to your bow.

First and foremost, he was highly competent in terms of his defensive workrate, positioning and ability to secure possession.

His team-mates remember him as someone who trained as he played, always wanting to win back the ball. Well, almost always. Malcolm Crosby and Denis Smith did remember fondly one of their first sessions with the team, during which the gentle 25-minute warm-up was greeted with some consternation by Mickey.

'Right, that's us finished, we're knackered,' he joked, immediately endearing himself to the new management team. But generally speaking, he trained hard. 'It was the only way he knew how to,' as Anton Rogan remembers, 'it was a great way to do it.' And from that foundation built on the training ground, Mickey consistently translated his defensive acumen and tenacity on to the pitch.

Former Oxford United youth development officer Les Taylor agreed wholeheartedly with that assessment: 'Mickey knew everything about playing midfield. If you're not tight on your man, you give them too much room to play. And he knew fine well that if you come up against a good player, they're only a good player if you let them be. If you come up against a player who is better than you, you'd better stop them.'

And stop them he did, more often than not winning his midfield duels against even the most impressive of opposition players.

Indeed, former Liverpool player and Oxford United manager Mark Lawrenson, a man who knows a thing or two about defending, remembers Mickey as a player who *'never* got pulled out of position, who *never* let you down'.

* * *

On top of these defensive qualities – in fact, because of them – Mickey was certainly a talented enabler of those around him, even if he was, by no stretch, a playmaker.

All players who are great with the ball need someone to win it for them and, as Peter Frain put it, 'knock it five or ten yards and get back into position'. To do the hard bit in the engine room of the midfield, to win the ball and then to give it to the players around them who can really play.

All creative midfielders who build their game on the taking of calculated attacking risks and find themselves out of position need dependable, trustworthy partners to cover and clean up after them. And those sorts of creative midfielders, often mavericks with adventurous streaks and hot heads, sometimes need someone to pull them back into the game, both positionally and mentally, when things aren't going their way.

That's what Mickey was at Oxford United. Particularly for Jim Magilton.

Magilton was one of Oxford United's finest ever midfielders. He was described by a poster on *Oxblogger* – an Oxford United fansite – as having 'possessed a touch and finesse which propped up an otherwise average mid-90s team'. Martin Tyler picked him out specifically in our conversation as a 'very gifted player on the ball, someone who would have fitted well in today's football'.

At first glance, these testimonies suggest Oxford were privileged to get Magilton from Liverpool in October of 1990, particularly given the Northern Irishman had to ask Liverpool manager Kenny Dalglish where exactly Oxford was when the offer came in. But looking a little deeper, Magilton was equally lucky to get Oxford – and Mickey as his midfield partner. When asked about that team and his pairing with Mickey, Magilton was quick to say that Mickey was his protector and someone who gave him an 'unbelievable platform to go and play'.

Magilton explained exactly what he meant, which whilst initially sounding subjective and hard to measure, gets to the core of one of Mickey's gifts as a team-mate and, later, as a coach. There were the obvious things. The things others have already said. 'He was like the Tasmanian Devil. He'd rattle after the ball.' But it was more than that. 'He just had this way of being able to lift you. A way of bollocking you. A way of encouraging you.' And how did he do that? 'He was just an unbelievable character. When you're in the trenches with characters like him, it's just amazing.'

Magilton is certainly not the only one to say something like this. Everyone we spoke to who played with or against Mickey said something along the lines of 'you would always want him on your team' or 'all of these naturally gifted match-winners, they are absolutely nothing without the likes of Mickey, who was *always* the first name on the team sheet'.

Such was Mickey's uplifting effect on players like Magilton, he even joked to the *Oxford Mail* some years later that all the time spent clearing up their mess in midfield probably accelerated his move into management by at least a couple of years.

And even when he was very occasionally left out of the team and as Mark Lawrenson's assistant, David Moss, put it, 'he was hurting, he was sulking inside', there he was five minutes before kick-off, 'going round and shaking the hands of the other players, encouraging them towards a good performance for the team and the club'.

So, just as Mickey played the game, doing the dirty work and providing a platform for others to go and shine, he took equally seriously his role as a positive influence on those around him, even when he wasn't selected to start.

* * *

Oh, and there is one more thing that needs recording when setting out the extent to which Mickey was more than just your average midfield bruiser.

Mickey didn't score goals very often. He recorded just over a handful in his entire career. But when he scored? Well, he scored some very, very good goals.

Oxford Radio's Jerome Sale recounted an infamous story from the Oxford football press corps. He told it second hand, on behalf of 'a guy from Fox FM'. The guy in question, a radio journalist, spent an afternoon watching Oxford United doing shooting practice at Shotover Park in Headington. He noted, quite quickly, that Mickey did, indeed, shoot over and always from the endearingly speculative distance of more or less 25 yards.

That same journalist was at Vicarage Road a matter of weeks later, in the early 1990s, watching Mickey shape up to shoot from that favourite distance of his. 'For Christ's sake, not another one,' he thought. Or at least he thought that until the ball nestled itself in the top corner of the Watford goal.

'That summed him up. He just wasn't put off by the fact 15 previous times he'd probably seen the shot go over the bar. He'd take it on again.'

That was Mickey. He took it on. And when it paid off, it really paid off. And he was known to remind people of that fact, too. In fact, he remembered every single time he'd found the net – admittedly there weren't many – and he enjoyed recounting them whenever he got the chance.

There is one video that Mickey was particularly fond of once he'd been introduced to smartphones and YouTube some years after the end of his playing career. It shows the highlights from Oxford United against Stockport County, a thumping 4-0 win at the Manor Ground in late February 1995 in the middle of a tight race for promotion against Sam Allardyce's Blackpool. Mickey was known to get the video out every now and then, narrating as he watched.

The ball bounces loose outside the area. Mickey, in that distinctive yellow top and his blue shorts pulled high around his waist, sprints into frame. The ball continues to bobble. Fans in the background shout 'shoot' or 'you've got to hit that'. And unlike players today, for whom it is made clear that such situations rarely result in goals and they should ignore the temptation accordingly, Mickey *does* shoot. He really hits it. The ball arrows into the back of the net, over the flailing keeper's head.

The Manor Ground explodes in that way stadiums do when goal-shy fan favourites pop up with a goal. Jim Magilton and David Rush throw themselves at Mickey. The commentator chimes in soon after with perfect timing: 'Mickey Lewis scores his goal for the season. Pure gold.'

'Should have played me up front,' Mickey used to mutter as he closed down the highlights video, slipped his phone back into his pocket and walked off into the distance.

* * *

So that was Mickey. The man Mark Lawrenson remembered as a 'Steady Eddie' who played with a mix of maturity and selflessness rare in the ego-driven world of professional football. The beloved midfield 'Mad Dog' with a thunderbolt or two in his back pocket. The midfield lynchpin who never let down his team-mates, fans or club.

Well, not quite *never*.

Former *Oxford Mail* sports editor Mark Edwards laughed as he talked us through the process he used to employ for the *Mail*'s star ratings. It was a simple system, from one to five. But the impact of those straightforward numbers was often significant. 'Players were so precious about what marks they got,' Edwards remembered. 'You wouldn't believe the amount of times people would complain.'

Naturally, Mickey saw this somewhat differently. Whenever a team-mate received a one – which Edwards notes was given out very rarely, only when someone was 'pretty abysmal' – Mickey took it upon himself to come up with a sheriff's bib which was to be worn in training by the unlucky recipient of the *Mail*'s ire until the next suitably poor performance was turned in.

Of course, you know where this is going. Mickey did eventually get his own one-star rating. It was towards the end of the season, which meant he ended up wearing his own sheriff's bib for about six months. But when Edwards suggested to him that such a humiliation must have been a nightmare, Mickey's reply was exactly as you'd expect: 'To be honest, I think one out of five was quite generous!'

Chapter Seven:

'He epitomised what a fan would do, if they were given the chance'

'He would have played in goal or made the tea if you asked him. And he would have loved every minute of it.'

Anonymous contributor 'Scotch Egg' on an
Oxford United fans' forum

EVERY TRUE football fan will be able to list the great players to have worn their club's shirt. The names they looked for first on the team sheet. The defenders who bled for the badge. The attackers who got them – and those around them – up and out of their seats.

But there is a special category within those shared club histories: the club man. The rare ones – ones who often committed the majority of their career to one club, who gave everything, on *and* off the pitch.

At Oxford United, Mickey was certainly one of these club men.

And so, it wasn't just his combative defensive qualities or his midfield partnership with Jim Magilton that enamoured Mickey to the Oxford faithful and cemented his 'Mad Dog' nickname through the late 1980s and across the 1990s. Nor was it his occasional outside-the-box rocket.

As long-serving Oxford United administrator Mick Brown remembers, Mickey developed a reputation, more or less as soon as he arrived at the Manor Ground, for working as hard around the club and the training ground as he did on the pitch: 'He was so energetic. Rain, shine, wind, snow. He was always there in his shorts and his waterproof, with his curly hair and his slight limp. He was always the heartbeat of whatever was going on.'

Oxford United's gregarious groundsman, Mick Moore, recalled with great fondness this exceptional thirst for hard work and being helpful:

> 'On the days when Oxford would be snowed over, Mickey would be out there filling a trailer of snow before anyone had half-filled one. He was as strong as an ox. If we had to put the frost protection sheets across the pitch, he would be the first one out there. He threw himself into everything.'

You'd be hard pressed to find many modern-day midfielders shovelling snow or laying down ice protection sheets at dawn. Unless, perhaps, the club's social media manager was nearby, camera at the ready.

Moore recalled another similar situation which, as per many of Mickey's endeavours, began with a post-match drink at the Manor Ground.

Mickey was in the supporters' club after a game, buying pints for those in his company and keeping them there for one more. He caught a conversation across the room about the next day's training session, a light post-match run-out which would take place on the stadium pitch. Most would pay it no mind and continue working through their pint. Mickey's mind, however, went straight to his friend Moore.

He knew that a played-on pitch needed a good hour's work in the evening and an hour's preparation the next day. It might be said, too, that he knew that excellence was founded on details and paying attention to things that most people ignore. Things he knew in part because of those cold early mornings, in the snow, the sun peeking over the Oxfordshire horizon, laughing away with Moore as they set down the frost sheets and shovelled the snow.

He shot across the room: 'Mooresy, you know training's on the pitch tomorrow? First thing. 10am.'

Mooresy didn't know. The manager hadn't told him. And so, after Mickey had given him the heads-up, Moore went straight to the manager and told him where to shove it.

* * *

Mickey's off-pitch, club man qualities extended far beyond his support for the groundstaff.

He understood that his responsibility to the club – and to the fans, who to Mickey really were the club – stretched beyond his performance on a Saturday afternoon.

Jerome Sale would stand outside the double doors of the Beech Road stand for Oxford Radio, asking players to do an interview:

> 'Mickey never turned us down. It's one of the reasons he became so popular. He was wholehearted. He'd give anything to anybody. He could communicate. And he'd always speak to us after a defeat. And because United lost a lot, we spoke a lot.'

Of course, such a willingness to communicate with the press after the match did sometimes lead Mickey to trouble. Chris Williams, a former member of the Oxford United communications team who is now general manager at Oxford City, recalls such an instance.

United were playing in the first round of the FA Cup in 1994 at the 250-seater Alfred Davis Memorial Ground in Marlow. Mickey, by that point 29 and one of the senior players in the squad, wasn't in the starting XI, settled instead on the bench. Presumably, the coaching staff did not think he would be needed for such a seemingly straightforward cup tie.

But non-league Marlow surprised everyone and became the first winners of the Littlewoods Pools Giant-Killing Award with a 2-0 victory. It was a defeat that the bubbly commentator described as 'far more disturbing than Frankenstein', sealed by two goals from bricklayer Don Caesar. Real name.

As the squad left the ground, Mickey was asked by some journalists why he didn't get on to the pitch. His response? 'Because I would have tried.'

Mickey surely meant exactly what he said. It was funny. Chris Williams remembered the moment with a chuckle. It was probably a totally fair assessment of his team-mates' performance. It was the perfect encapsulation of his relationship with the club he'd come to love and a fanbase which had come to love him back. Still, it probably didn't land that well on the training ground the following day.

But, you know, more than one person did say to us that they 'can't ever remember Mickey getting in trouble'.

* * *

Slightly pointed post-match quips aside, Mickey ultimately knew several things to be true.

He knew his worth to his team was based first on him running more than his opposite man, on his willingness to make tackles others would shy away from and his reliability in getting the ball quickly to the ones who could make things happen. He knew, as well, the importance of demonstrating the same level of commitment off the pitch, in the graft and teamwork required to keep the pitches playable, to keep the lights on, to keep the fans singing, to keep a club running.

Beneath all that was the same pure, unshowy hard work that had marked him out back in the West Brom academy, in his early training sessions with the West Brom first team and in his outings for the England age group sides.

Bursting lungs. Dripping sweat. That's what endeared Mickey so much to everyone associated with the club and particularly the fans.

And it is the fans who write the obituaries, who campaign for the statues and who turn up to the testimonials. They sing the names, make the myths and pass it all on to the next generation. Without their love, a player will never mean much to a club. So, there is no more potent compliment than that of Jerome Sale's of Oxford Radio when he reflected that Mickey 'epitomised what the fans wanted players to show, to go down fighting, to look like they care'.

This, we think, begins to answer our guiding question: why were all those people at the Kassam Stadium for Mickey's memorial match in October 2021? And why did he have such a profound, outsized impact on all those he met?

'In many aspects,' Sale continued, 'he epitomised what a fan would do, if they were given the chance.'

SECTION ONE PART II:

GUARANTEEING A PERFORMANCE (THE GAME OWES YOU NOTHING)

Chapter Eight

'Only mad dogs and Englishmen go out in the midday sun'

MICKEY FIRST tried to retire from playing in 1996, aged 31.

The timing made sense: he had just played his part in helping navigate a sprint finish to promotion in the 1995/96 season. A promotion that would return Oxford back to what was by this point called the First Division or, alternatively, the tier below the Premier League.

That success had not been inevitable. Far from it. After an opening day win against Chesterfield, Oxford United only won three times in their next 14. They didn't win away until January, when they recorded a 2-0 win at Burnley.

And then, seemingly out of the blue, thanks in no small part to a shift in that curious beast momentum, a late February win at Carlisle changed everything. After that match in Cumbria, Oxford basically couldn't stop winning.

By the penultimate game of the season, Sam Allardyce's Blackpool, a side who had appeared out of reach even just a few games prior, were overtaken. Oxford's automatic promotion was secured on the final day in front of a bumper crowd at the Manor Ground.

The *Oxford Mail* archive still carries an excellent summary of those remarkable few months, complete with a wonderful set of photos and an anecdote on the psychology of a promotion race.

After a key game against pacesetters Blackpool in early April, Allardyce's assistant, Phil Brown – who would go on to give that famous Hull City on-pitch team talk at Manchester City, now immortalised by Jimmy Bullard's parody – had said that he was 'sure Oxford would do well in the play-offs'. As Oxford's Mike Ford went on to note, it was 'the added bit of incentive we may have needed' to ultimately go on and pip them at the last.

Quite brilliantly, Ford apparently sent Brown and the Blackpool team a postcard from the beach in Majorca, ahead of the first leg of the play-off match that Blackpool, rather than Oxford, would need to play. It read: 'To Phil, good luck in the play-offs, love Oxford United.'

With the postcard sent and the promotion secured, Mickey had the opportunity to bow out in style, as one of Oxford United's most celebrated players. Indeed, as the club website 'Dream Team' section puts it today: 'If ever there was a Mr Oxford United, Mickey Lewis would be the prime candidate.'

And so it was, as United began the 1996/97 season and consolidated their place in the second tier over the following two campaigns, Mickey was gaining his first coaching experience with the youth team.

He had wanted to be a coach for a long time. When he'd been asked in his introductory interview for the Derby fan magazine if he had any ambitions for the end of his playing career, he'd said: 'I hope it's a long way off, but I'd like to earn a place on the coaching side of football.'

And whilst he had also mentioned to that Derby magazine that he might one day like to open a restaurant, he was clearly excited about the move. Malcolm Crosby and Denis Smith, who observed his approach to the youth team, went as far as to wonder whether he was 'on some sort of happy pill'. And the *Oxford Mail* wrote at the time:

> 'Only mad dogs and Englishmen go out in the midday sun and one Mad Dog, Oxford United's tough-tackling midfielder Mickey Lewis, is out on the training ground at noon most days in a new and challenging capacity.
>
> 'Lewis jumped at the opportunity to coach the kids. "It's a new challenge for me. I'll be concentrating on coaching the youth team and will do most of my training with the kids. I see this as a first step on the ladder to coaching and maybe management."'

Few were surprised by the way in which he made the transition from pitch to dugout.

As several people who had played with Mickey put it, he was a man who understood intimately the connection between time spent on and around the training ground, and performances and results on the pitch. Because of that, he had a range of talents at his disposal: hard work, selflessness, always having an eye out for those who needed a hand up, an arm round the shoulder, or a good laugh to get them over a poor performance or a defeat.

Martin Tyler has watched more football than most, and he saw such a background as a critical factor in coaching or managerial success. In fact, he suggested to us that Mickey, being a player who wasn't as naturally talented as many of his team-mates and who had to work hard on his skills, was well suited to life on the touchline. 'I think you have to have been a player,' as Tyler put it, 'who has had to work really hard at your game, and suffer a lot, to truly appreciate it.'

None of that is to say Mickey was happy to be leaving his playing duties entirely behind.

In that same *Oxford Mail* article announcing his transition to the youth team coaching role, he did finish with the note that he'd 'always be available for selection for the first team'. And it proved to be a prescient addendum.

* * *

Oxford had once more been relegated back to the third tier of English football by the 1999/2000 season, succumbing to their fate on the last day of the 1998/99 campaign, finishing 23rd.

And as that return to the third tier began, Oxford were grappling with a profoundly shaky financial position, question marks over the future of the club's ground and the expectation of a takeover by London hotelier Firoz Kassam.

Amidst this chaos and setting aside the signing of non-contract forms at local side Banbury, Mickey, now 34, had transitioned seamlessly on to the club's staff. No doubt in addition to his unofficial groundsman duties, he was soon driving the team bus, deputising for the physio and taking seriously his duties as a de facto social secretary, in charge of club karaoke nights.

But even recognising this unerring commitment to the cause – a cause that was becoming more difficult by the day – few could have predicted what Mickey would be asked come September.

Oxford were drawn against Premier League Everton in the League Cup, a competition now sponsored by Worthington.

It should have been an exciting occasion and an opportunity for Oxford's players to test themselves against some of the best in the country. But the club were woefully short of match-fit first-team players. So, as the *Oxford Mail* put it at the time: 'Injury-hit Oxford have put youth team coach Mickey Lewis on standby to face Everton in the Worthington Cup tonight.' It was quite a remarkable state of affairs, given the report went on to note that 'Lewis has not started a first-team match in years'.

Years later, Mickey reflected that, even when training with the first team the day before the game, he'd never actually expected to play. He was convinced someone would come through and recover. But such was the extent of the injury crisis that he was soon off standby and on the bench for the first leg.

The game – played out at the Manor Ground in front of just over 7,000 people – ended in a 1-1 draw, with goals for Everton's Danny Cadamarteri and Oxford's Matt Murphy. Again, the *Mail* provides wonderful colour: 'Everton were given a big scare as Oxford's Dad's Army went on the offensive.'

But it was the second leg that perfectly bookended Mickey's United career.

Only 10,000 people were at Goodison Park for a match that Oxford would win 1-0, thanks to an early Joey Beauchamp goal.

One fan's match account on the excellent archival source of *toffeeweb.com* lamented 'another experiment in squad rotation for the Everton players, in the much-maligned Worthington Cup'. Contributor and presumably long-suffering Everton fan Steve Bickerton was even more cutting: 'We had a makeshift team playing makeshift football, acting as if it was a Wednesday night in the Pontins Premier Division.' The Pontins Premier Division being the league in which the reserve squads of England's top teams played at the time.

But none of that should devalue the fact that Mickey, having whirred his body back into action, stepped in at centre-half for his first start in a couple of years and gave what more than one observer described as the 'performance of his career'. Even as former England youth stars Francis Jeffers and Kevin Campbell came on at half-time to help Everton chase the game, Mickey completed an integral defensive performance at the heart of one of the club's great cup nights.

It was a big 'well done to the walking wounded heroes of Oxford United' from the *Mail*. And there was a special mention for Mickey and the 'romantic tale [of his] remarkable comeback'.

As the *Mail* asked: 'What is a three-year lay-off to a seasoned, enthusiastic old war horse?'

Mickey apparently enjoyed the match so much he spent the rest of the evening wondering aloud whether he'd stepped away too soon from playing.

* * *

It would soon transpire that a couple of Worthington Cup appearances were far from the extent of Mickey's first-team involvement that season. But not, perhaps, for the reasons Mickey expected in the beer-soaked glow of those post-Everton celebrations.

Oxford's return to the third tier had started poorly, giant-killing at Goodison Park aside. A run of seven losses in eight spelled the end for Malcolm Shotton – who had been in charge for Oxford's famous League Cup win in 1986 in what was increasingly feeling like a different era – and his assistant, Mark Harrison.

That decision wasn't particularly controversial or unpopular. In another *Mail* article from the time, Jon Murray noted that 'in nearly 20 years of reporting on football, I can't ever remember a manager more hated by some of his players'. It was a tale of ruling by fear and intimidation, and a breakdown in relations with the board. A tale that a fair number of fans across England will recognise all too acutely today.

The injury crisis that had led to Mickey's selection in the team against Everton was persisting, which was making matters worse. The possibility of a disastrous, second successive relegation quickly began to feel very real.

And so, Mickey was the short-term caretaker manager appointment in October 1999 that the board felt would lift the fans and players for just long enough to keep them in the division and allow them to work out a more sustainable long-term plan. It was the late 1990s version of modern owners making the call to a club legend, like Newcastle United did – unsuccessfully – with former striker Alan Shearer in 2009.

Mickey was soon overseeing a long unbeaten run through the late autumn and into winter, with good wins away at Alan Pardew's Reading and also Notts County. And he was clearly enjoying himself, too, embracing the sort of big decisions caretakers often avoid. One report on that win at Reading describes how he 'dumped Premier League target Paul Powell and Peter Fear on the bench and blooded young Ross Weatherstone'. It was a debut that Weatherstone described in post-match interviews as the 'best day of my life', whilst also referring to his hometown club Reading as 'the scum'. He subsequently admitted he'd recorded and re-watched the game six times.

It seems fair to conclude from Weatherstone's exuberance that Mickey's enthusiasm was proving to be infectious. Midfielder Matt Murphy certainly thought so, telling the *Oxford Mail* that 'there isn't a single bloke in our dressing room that doesn't want [Mickey] to get the job full-time'. And the *Mail*'s David Pritchard reflected along similar lines:

> 'Psychologists talk about radiators or drains. Well, in the job I had, you find out a lot about people when they lose. Mickey was honest when we lost, but he'd give you something to hold on to, some sort of positivity. That's surely what he could do for the players as well.'

He seemed to be managing upwards with some success, too.

Groundsman Mick Moore remembers one particular afternoon during Mickey's caretaker tenure when Oxford had lost and the backroom staff had gathered in one of the stadium bars to commiserate. Knowing Mickey, the commiserations were surely far from wretched. There was likely some excitement in the air, a hopefulness about a new era despite the frustrations of the day.

But losing is never good news for a football club. And so, when the owner, hotelier Firoz Kassam, burst into the bar, beers went behind backs and a hush came over the room. Until Mickey cut through all of it, that is.

'Oh, Mr Kassam! Hello mate. Come on in, have a drink. Let's chat about the game. What's coming next? We're at home next weekend. Now, what I'm thinking is …'

Moore, one of those to carry on drinking his beer as Mr Kassam arrived, recalled Mickey's words 'totally calming what could have been an awkward, dangerous situation'.

So, the support Mickey had across the club was palpable. And this seemed to be the primary reason, as well as continuity and Mickey's obvious love for Oxford, that journalists like David Wynne-Jones were using their local newspaper columns to advocate for Mickey getting the job full-time. Well, that and him being the 'cheaper option' too.

But while the situation seemed an ideal one for the board – with a successful start for a bona fide fan favourite – they continued their search for a permanent manager. Journalist Russell Kempson reported at the time on the remarkable number of applications and curriculum vitae of 'vastly greater substance' than Mickey's that were flooding into the club.

Mickey wasn't deterred. In fact, he responded to the speculation on which Kempson was reporting in quite bullish fashion:

> 'Of course, I want the manager's job and it's no big deal when I see the big names being lined up as possible candidates. It's something of a dressing room joke now. Until our chairman Firoz Kassam makes his mind up, I'll keep enjoying it.'

* * *

Unfortunately for Mickey and those who were so invested in his success, the good times didn't last.

As is so often the case in English football, the busy Christmas period, with matches coming thick and fast, was unforgiving. In fact, after a 3-2 away defeat at Burnley in late December, Oxford picked up a solitary point in the six matches that followed. During that run, they conceded 15 goals and scored only twice – not a record Mickey would have enjoyed as a man who had built a career on his defensive qualities.

He would later acknowledge his youth and inexperience, and suggest he wasn't as ready for the responsibility as he might have felt and suggested at the time. But back in early 2000, the pressure of his side's festive downturn didn't change Mickey, at least not outwardly.

The *Oxford Mail*'s Mark Edwards recounted a Friday evening before one of Mickey's games in charge, during which he received a team news tip-off from a fellow journalist, who was covering that Saturday's opposition.

As a sign of enduring respect to his profession and his colleagues, Edwards wouldn't share much of the detail. But, in short, a star player who'd been injured for six months was making an unexpected return.

Edwards had a dilemma. The intel seemed solid, but Mickey had surely already picked the team. A week's preparation was in the bank.

Ultimately, Edwards decided to phone Mickey to relay the information. It was, as he'd expected, too late to make any major changes. And the player did go on to both start and play a starring role in inflicting defeat on Mickey's Oxford side.

Yet, there Mickey was after the match, searching for Edwards in the post-match melee. He took him to the manager's office and gave him a box of beer. 'Thanks for letting me know. You didn't have to do that.'

By February, with no sign of results improving, it seemed almost inevitable that Mickey would step aside. And so it was that, after 22 games in the dugout, he was replaced by former Oxford United manager Denis Smith and largely returned to his previous duties elsewhere in the club.

The club's official history is relatively blunt about Mickey's time in charge. 'After initially steadying the ship, it was felt that a more experienced manager was needed, as the team's fortunes nosedived.'

Ultimately, the season ended with Oxford in 20th position out of 24 teams, avoiding relegation to the dreaded fourth tier of English football – a league Oxford had not played in since 1984 – by a single point.

* * *

As winter turned to spring in 2000, more or less a year after Mickey had been placed in charge of the club he'd called home for over a decade, and following a brief stint as assistant to another caretaker manager after Denis Smith's resignation, he was leaving.

The exact circumstances of the exit seem to differ depending on who you speak to. One person, who didn't want to be quoted, suggested the new Kassam ownership drove Mickey out. Perhaps to freshen things up.

That is, of course, conjecture. But Mickey, 35 at the time, himself told the *Oxford Mail* that he 'felt a bit cheated by the people that were running the club at the time', having 'been there for ages and done everything [he could] to keep the club going'. A good number of fans clearly agreed, writing letters to the city's newspaper complaining that the decision was a mistake and a disgrace.

None of this changed the fact it was time for Mickey to leave. So, after what was apparently a legendary leaving party, Mickey moved into a job as a player-coach for the city's non-league side, Oxford City. It was a major coup for manager Paul Lee, with Mickey committing to help out the young squad – which had an average age of 21 – on and off the pitch.

At the same time, Mickey also began what would become a two-decade-long and immensely successful association with the University of Oxford first XI, known as the 'Blues'.

Mickey said in an interview later in his career that he'd never had any intention of dropping out of the professional game. But he also reflected in that same interview that the move 'allowed [him] to learn a great deal about all the sides of a football club'.

And so, if Mickey's transition from the pitch to a top-level dugout had undoubtedly suffered a setback, life beyond Oxford United soon seemed to be falling into place as he began piecing together a post-playing career that was allowing him to both stay in football and stay in the Oxford area he'd come to call home.

Until, that is, America came calling.

Chapter Nine

Dream Baby Dream

DES MOINES, Iowa, is one of the most significant cities in American politics. That makes it one of the most significant political cities in the world.

The city is the centre of gravity for the Iowa Caucus – a hyper-localised set of elections that's the first of the votes through which the Democrats and Republicans choose their presidential candidates.

So, once every four years, and particularly for the party that's not in power, Des Moines becomes a place in which dreams can be realised or shattered. A place that can catapult even the most unknown of senators to the Oval Office or send political veterans back to their smaller-horizoned desks elsewhere.

As the *New York Times* commented during the 2008 election campaign: 'If you have any desire to witness presidential candidates in the most close-up and intimate of settings, there is arguably no better place to go than Des Moines.'

But what you don't hear *quite* as often is that Iowa is a part of Mickey Lewis's story, too.

Yet there Mickey was, perhaps buoyed by the memories of his return to the Oxford first team for the cup triumph over Everton and a little wounded as his time on the Yellows' coaching staff came to an end, making something of an unusual career decision. Unusual, at least, for 2000.

He entered a no-man's land between the end of a serious playing career and a full hanging-up of the boots. The same no-man's land that today sees players drop down into the depths of England's non-league pyramid as a player-coach or head off to Japan or Saudi Arabia to keep the fire burning or the cash flowing for just a little longer. And he decided to do so in the American Midwest.

Few bookmakers would have predicted the move. Football is a small world, though, and friend and former team-mate Dave Penney made contact with Mickey as soon as he'd heard the news that his association with Oxford United had come to an end. Dave was now with Doncaster Rovers, whose chief executive had just left to go and head up Iowa's premier 'soccer' team, Des Moines Menace.

Dave got in touch to tell Mickey that the Menace wanted an experienced pro on the coaching staff – and in the centre of midfield, too. Dave thought it sounded like a bit of fun. So, would Mickey do it? Not one to agonise over decisions, Mickey was on the next plane.

* * *

The state of US soccer at the turn of the millennium was some way short of the game more and more Americans are coming to love today as Beckham, Messi and friends cruise towards the 2026 US, Canada and Mexico World Cup. And Mickey was making a move from near the top of English football to the Premier Development League, a division many levels below the top tier of US soccer. So, he was surely expecting something of a culture shock as he touched down on American soil.

If Mickey received any sort of pre-arrival pack or any information about what was ahead of him, the team names were likely the first sign that things were going to be a little different. Laurie Calloway, who managed the Menace during Mickey's time with the club, left in 2003 to join the Syracuse Salty Dogs. Des Moines have at various points in their relatively brief existence competed against the Kalamazoo Kingdom, the Austin Lone Stars, Rochester Raging Rhinos, the Rockford Raptors and the Sioux Falls Spitfire. The best of the lot? The Thunder Bay Chill.

But as Mickey's time in Iowa played out, amusing team names were quickly far down the list of curiosities.

Nobody who we interviewed could confirm whether or not Mickey was ever paid by his Des Moines employers. That is perhaps why the club's quite extensive Wikipedia history, complete with a detailed summary of their early 2000s success, makes no mention of the arrival or contribution of their star Englishman. Nor does the website's long list of Menace players who've come from or gone on to bigger and better things.

As for the football itself? Even before a ball was kicked, things were a little different to the ever-richer English football back home. The Menace's home games were played at a local school sports stadium, belonging to the 2,000-student Valley High public school. Away matches were often eight or more hours away on a bus.

And whilst the club's official history notes that 2002 was 'a banner year for Des Moines' in which the club recorded an unbeaten season, won their league by 20 points and secured a trip to the US Open Cup, Mickey had somewhat less luck during his stint in the 2001 season.

The promotion rules and league structures at the time seem to have been changing regularly, but whatever the rules exactly were, Mickey's Menace side finished second in the Heartland Division, missing out on a top spot that went to the now-defunct Sioux Falls Spitfire. They did qualify for the national semi-finals, on account of the finals being held in Des Moines, but they lost 5-1 to eventual champions Westchester Flames.

But did Mickey complain about any of these oddities? Did he rue the chain of events that had taken him from the precipice of becoming the permanent manager of his beloved Oxford United to middle-of-nowhere USA? Not for a second. Dave Penney tells of Mickey's response to the experience.

'He was so easy-going and just so happy to be playing football. He would say "Oh, it doesn't matter. It doesn't. Yeah, there was a bit of a [pay] dispute, but I wasn't out of pocket. Nah. It was fine."

'And then he'd just tell me about the hilarious times they had on the road, in the team digs, at the middle-of-nowhere Midwestern bars. I asked him, "What did you do on those long coach rides?" "What do you mean? Just get the cards and a crate of beer out," he'd say. Easy. Typical Mick.'

He was equally willing to see the funny side of the situation in an interview he gave to West Brom's Laurie Rampling some years later. 'John Wayne lived out there and I went past his house! That's what you do in Iowa, you go and look at people's houses,' Mickey recalled.

* * *

Alas, the adventure was short-lived. The Menace's shirt sponsors at the time were a chain of convenience stores called Kum & Go. And that could serve as a neat summary of Mickey's time there. Brief. He came. He went.

So it was that Des Moines became the unlikely place that Mickey's playing career truly ended.

After making his mark at West Bromwich Albion, solidifying his reputation at Derby County and securing club legend status at Oxford United, a fun but short-lived stint with the Menace was the final confirmation Mickey needed: he was no longer a 20-something 'Mad Dog'. Even if he was still able to mix it with the best of them whenever it was time for a crate of beer, a pack of cards and eight hours on a Greyhound bus, it was time to say goodbye to the pitch, move 30 yards sideways and say hello to the coaches' dugout.

None of that is to say that he went out of the game in disgrace. Mickey's time in Iowa was not like that of the politicians who go there and find their careers ending in shame. Instead, he approached his time in Des Moines as he approached everything, with an infectious enthusiasm and a commitment to getting absolutely everything out of himself and the opportunity in front of him, on and off the pitch.

And once he'd finished, he moved on to the next challenge, setting about ensuring his post-Iowa life was full of its own adventure and a little bit of glory, too.

All revolving around football, of course.

Chapter Ten

Mad Dog to top dog?

'We want to be a passing team. But not a passing team that goes nowhere. I don't want us to pass just for the sake of it.'

Mickey Lewis on his footballing philosophy

AS 2001 was turning to 2002 – and as Mickey was entering the second half of his 30s – he was back from Des Moines. In returning to the Oxford area, he was facing the realities of the fact he was no longer professionally associated with his beloved Oxford United. What, then, would be next?

Given Mickey's success as a young academy player at West Brom – breaking into the first team as one of the club's youngest ever debutants – he had not completed school through to 18. And, as it was for most footballers at the time, he had not earned wages during his playing career that guaranteed a lifetime of comfort. Facing this situation, some of Mickey's playing peers flourished. Others undoubtedly floundered.

When assessing which of these categories best fits Mickey, there are a whole host of metrics to suggest that Mickey flourished. He began to assemble a paid coaching career on his return from Des Moines that would largely keep him in the professional game and doing what he loved for the next two decades. He impacted hundreds if not thousands of players – and particularly young players – as he did so.

But we do also want to recognise here that what follows is not straightforwardly positive. Mickey's was not an ascent to the pinnacle of English football as a coach or manager. He had struggles during his post-playing career: losing jobs, getting temporary jobs, working several jobs at once. He had to be patient in his pursuit of a role not only befitting of his talent but also of his desire, in many ways ahead of its time, to take care of his family.

So how to balance these two realities against each other? How to decide if Mickey's post-playing career was a flourish or a flounder?

We think the fact there is such an array of highs and lows in the pages that follow is exactly the point and a crucial part of answering the question posed at the beginning of this book, the question of what impact Mickey had on all the people around him. In the face of knockbacks, tough-to-swallow results and even firings, Mickey's passion for the game and his commitment to sharing that passion with his players never really seemed to dwindle at all.

And in that, the truth of Mickey's story, and his legacy, begins to reveal itself.

* * *

Mickey returned first to his coaching duties at the university and at Oxford City, picking up work as well at nearby non-league side Slough Town, having missed out on the manager's job at Aylesbury United.

The first-team boss at City, Paul Lee, recalls just how hard Mickey had to work in that period to properly establish himself away from the playing side of the game: 'He used to work in the early morning delivering newspapers. He was also working as a first-team coach for Eddie Denton at Slough Town. He was up every single day at 5am.'

It wasn't just delivering newspapers that he juggled with his responsibilities on the training ground. He'd wash the kit. He'd meet with the youth development coaches. He'd do 100 other things for which he was probably only partly responsible and most likely not paid. Probably forgetting breakfast or lunch as he did so.

All this soon became a schedule that would have broken many. It was surely a different experience to the one his old team-mate Jim Magilton would soon embark upon as the manager of Championship side Ipswich Town.

And this wasn't a fleeting moment of gruelling work in an ultimately comfortable coaching career. We witnessed Mickey washing the Oxford City kit after a university training session that finished at 10pm on a Monday, well over a decade after his early days balancing Oxford City and Slough Town.

It's no surprise really, considering this context, that Mickey's car was a famous joke amongst those who worked with him. Kelvin Thomas, Northampton Town chairman and one of

Mickey's closest friends, described the trusty Peugeot he drove at the time as 'unbelievably messy, with footballs everywhere, perhaps 30 in there at any one time'. Or, as Paul Lee put it, a little more bluntly: 'It was a dustbin.'

Mickey was apparently heartbroken when he finally had to send the car to the scrapyard after the best efforts of his former United team-mate and amateur mechanic Les Phillips to keep it on the road finally ran out of road themselves.

* * *

This period of Mickey's life, whilst undoubtedly challenging, did allow him the space to develop as a coach.

Given the circumstances in which Mickey had taken his first youth team coaching role and then the caretaker management at Oxford back in the late 1990s – that is, as a club legend known for his talents in the centre of midfield – he had probably not had a great deal of time to think clearly about his coaching philosophy. He had surely relied on an understanding of the game from his perspective as a player and the personal relationships he had developed as a result of over a decade in yellow.

So, once back from Des Moines and away from Oxford United, Mickey could begin to more consciously develop the principles from which he would coach across the rest of his career. He worked through his badges, as you'd expect. And he had time to draw more consciously on his lessons and experiences from a playing journey that had wound from the pitches of the Birmingham youth leagues – a time in which he'd been supported and encouraged to work hard by those at home – through to the First Division.

As he worked across Oxfordshire, the result soon revealed itself to be a rare mix of philosophical, psychological and tactical adeptness. Most who worked with or trained under Mickey around this time in his life recall his ability to combine his extensive footballing experience with a relentless positivity and enthusiasm that meant everyone who was on the pitch wanted to be there and wanted to work hard, whether an eight-year-old or a future first-team pro. Most also remember a remarkable clarity of communication, combined with a genuine care for the players in his charge.

Tristan Lewis worked with Mickey in several contexts across his coaching career and he described the experience of being on the training pitch together:

> 'I never saw a session plan. But it didn't matter. [The sessions] were always right. For the person, the player, the level. They were always intense. Always fun. He believed training was about putting bricks in a person's wall. Every session you were putting a new brick in the wall. Oh, and if someone was a prick in a session, he made sure they were dealt with. So, no one really ever did fuck about. The respect for him was profound.'

Mickey's wife, Suzanne, added a point of clarification to Tristan's comment. She noted that Mickey did, in fact, work on plans ahead of time. He just wrote them on scraps of paper before committing them to memory, not needing to take the plans with him. There is evidence to support this, too. Those scraps are still popping up all over their house, a testament to Mickey's meticulous approach to his coaching responsibilities.

But the existence or otherwise of developed plans is not the point. Plan or no plan, scrap paper or no scrap paper, the effect was clear. 'You worked your socks off for him, you'd run through a brick wall for him.' So said former Oxford United defender Andy Whing. 'He drove standards all the time. If he had one choice word, you'd listen to him.'

* * *

Mickey got another chance to put his increasingly developed coaching principles into practice in the professional game – a return to which he admitted he was hankering after – at the start of the 2005/06 campaign.

He had just turned 40 and he left behind his commitments at Oxford City, Slough Town, the Reading academy, the local Oxford school circuit and the university to join his good friend Dave Penney's coaching team at Doncaster Rovers.

Penney had been at Doncaster as a player and then a manager since the turn of the century, lifting the club out of the Conference and into England's third tier, League One. He'd established the youth section, too. Mickey would be joining to work with Penney at first-team level, whilst also leading the club's reserves.

It was an interesting move. Combined with his decision to head to Des Moines a few years prior, it suggests he was – at least at that stage in his career – willing to travel and relocate in search of professional opportunity.

And whilst the time Mickey spent with Penney in Doncaster was relatively short-lived, given the two of them left at the end of the 2005/06 season, the pair enjoyed a healthy amount of success.

In fact, their efforts in the regular season returned a respectable eighth-placed League One finish. In a league that included Brentford, Nottingham Forest and Bournemouth – how things can change – Doncaster fell just two points short of Swansea, who took the final play-off position.

But, more memorably, the two close friends oversaw one of Doncaster's most famous cup runs, reaching the last eight of the League Cup, which was then sponsored by Carling.

Their second-round match against Manchester City, played in front of just over 8,000 fans in late September 2005, was goalless after regular time. When City's one-time England striker Darius Vassell scored a penalty on 95 minutes, it looked as though the Premier League side would be dumping out Doncaster with little more than a minor scare. It would have been the sort of nondescript cup tie that was forgotten as quickly as it had happened.

But high drama soon followed.

City's Nedum Onuoha was sent off for a tackle that broke Doncaster keeper Andy Warrington's leg. In his autobiography, *Kicking Back,* Onuoha protests his innocence, chalking it up as a refereeing error that punished his over-excited and rare foray into the opposition box.

But Onuoha was gone and, with just two minutes left of extra time, it was Doncaster's turn for a penalty, striker Michael McIndoe converting it past David James to take the game to a penalty shoot-out. Doncaster's substitute keeper, debutant Jan Budtz, was the hero and Rovers moved on to the third round.

Doncaster went on to make light work of Gillingham. A cup run was, by that point, officially on.

And if the Gillingham result had given all those associated with Doncaster permission to dream, everything soon became a little more real. Because the game that followed the wins against City and then Gillingham – against Premier League Aston Villa in the fourth round – was even more remarkable.

One glance at the Villa team sheet shows the gulf in class Penney, Mickey and Co. were dealing with: Thomas Sørensen, Olof Mellberg, Liam Ridgewell, Gareth Barry, James Milner, Milan Baroš, Juan Pablo Ángel. It was one of Villa's strongest sides in recent memory. No wonder, then, that *avfchistory.co.uk* describes the result – a glorious 3-0 win for Doncaster – as a 'humiliating defeat'.

If under-fire Villa manager David O'Leary could count on any goodwill from players or fans at Villa Park prior to the match, it was certainly extinguished by the time referee Mike Dean blew the final whistle. As *avfchistory.co.uk* puts it: 'The only outstanding questions were when [he would go] and whether he would finally take the chairman with him.'

No one at Doncaster would have cared about any of that. Penney and Mickey were flying and, just before Christmas, it was time for the quarter-final against Arsène Wenger's Arsenal.

Ten thousand packed into Doncaster's ground for the occasion. And though Wenger played a few youngsters, he showed both the cup and his opposition some respect: Robin van Persie led the Arsenal line, with Gilberto Silva in the centre of midfield. In fact, it was virtually the same Arsenal team that won against Real Madrid at the Santiago Bernabéu a couple of months later.

It was another wildly entertaining cup game. The type of cup game fans of lower-league sides still talk about in pubs and chip shops years later.

Penney and Mickey's side took the lead in the fourth minute – Michael McIndoe again – before Quincy Owusu-Abeyie's equaliser, a deflected strike from outside the box.

Doncaster retook the lead in extra time through Paul Green, only to be cruelly denied in the very last minute of the 120 by Brazilian international Gilberto Silva. Arsenal won the shoot-out 3-1, leaving Penney, Mickey and all those associated with the League One club to dream of visiting Wembley another day or in another life.

That evening's result wasn't the only thing Penney and Mickey were left to rue.

Mickey and wife Suzanne had just settled into a house on the outskirts of Doncaster. He and Penney had just overseen the club's best season in half a century. And Mickey had personally masterminded a league-winning campaign with the reserve team. Yet, in the summer of 2006, it was time for Penney and Mickey to leave.

Why? The club's statement expressed 'great regret', going on to suggest that 'Dave feels he has taken the club as far as he can and Doncaster Rovers will not stand in his way in achieving his ambitions'.

No one we spoke to suggested Mickey was considered for the top job. The departure became a moment of refresh for Doncaster, as much as it did Penney. But with a typical stoicism and perhaps masking a deeper frustration at the lack of control Mickey had over his own career at that moment, Mickey told the press that it was 'a shame that we couldn't have carried it on'.

So, Mickey and Suzanne were soon moving back to Oxfordshire. And Mickey was once again grappling with the harsh realities of trying to build a sustainable coaching career in what was becoming an increasingly brutal industry. An industry in which the divide between the haves and have-nots was growing by the day.

A frantic portfolio of work followed once more. Mickey was soon doing driving jobs again, delivering mail across Oxfordshire four days a week. He was back with the university side, working at Abingdon Town and coaching various local youth teams as well.

As he put it at the time to the *Oxford Mail*: 'It's manic at the moment and I'm keeping my options open. I have seen some coaching jobs and sent in my CV, but nothing has come up. I'm not tied to anything. But I'm working seven days a week.'

* * *

On one early winter morning driving for the *Mail*, Mickey went down a cul-de-sac but then span the wheels as he backed out. He revved the engine to try and power the car out of this particular moment of bother. It was only after a few moments – and after it was too late – that he realised he was cutting up somebody's garden and spraying mud all over their living room window.

Such a moment might have brought another retired footballer to a moment of pause. A moment to reflect on the present trajectory of his life. Not for Mickey. He chuckled to himself, completed his delivery round and then circled back round to the house to repair the garden and clean up the windows.

So, through all these ups and downs in this early period of his coaching career, he was continuing to live and work as he'd played – working hard and with dedication to the task at hand but maintaining an unerring ability to see the best in everything and everyone around him. It was an approach that had and would continue to inspire so many.

And it was perhaps this enduring attitude that soon saw him rewarded with another shot at the job he wanted more than any other.

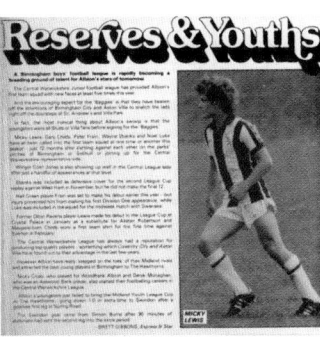

MICKY LEWIS

Mickey made a name for himself as a teenager whilst playing amateur football in Birmingham. He was soon snapped up by West Brom.

Mickey would ultimately be awarded his first professional contract in 1981, aged 16, and make his first team debut that same year. But none of that stopped him enjoying success with the Baggies' youth team.

A Report from Brett Gibbons on young Albion success in the 43rd Pforzheim Tournamant

▲ The victorious squad celebrate after retaining the magnificent trophy. Director Cliff Edwards is on hand to add his congratulations.

◀ Carl Addis, Andy Lacey, Micky Lewis and Kevin Keys have their own celebration.

Mickey burst into the West Brom first team aged just 16. He quickly left his mark on some of the country's best midfielders.

A photo of Mickey playing for West Brom, taken by a local photographer and sent to kitman Dave Matthews. The message reads: 'Keep this or pass it on to the lad. It's the first time I've got a decent shot of Mick[e]y in action. This was v West Ham – he did well.'

From late 1981 through to his departure for Derby in 1984, Mickey played over 30 times for the West Brom first team. Many at the club were sure they had a future international in their ranks.

Mickey wasn't a big footballer. But what he lacked in stature he made up for in bloody-minded competitiveness.

In the summer of 1982, aged 17, Mickey represented England at a youth tournament in Cannes. As his hair gives away, he's four in from the left on the back row.

The Derby squad that Mickey joined from West Brom, for a fee just shy of £30,000. Mickey is on the front row, three in from the left. Steve McClaren sits just right of the manager, Arthur Cox.

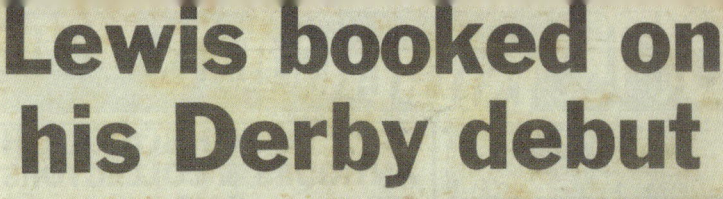

Lewis booked on his Derby debut

Mickey was booked within two minutes of his professional debut, in the League Cup for West Brom in 1981. He repeated the feat on debut for Derby three years later.

DERBY COUNTY were today without skipper Kenny Burns, who is still under treatment for a hamstring strain and missed his first match of the season.

Steve Powell moved into the back four for the visit of Wigan Athletic, with Mickey Lewis taking his place in midfield for his Rams debut.

Kevin Taylor was restored in midfield at the expense of Paul Richardson.

Wigan's one doubt on their first-ever visit was cleared when Graham Barrow was passed fit.

Wigan kicked off playing towards the Normanton End, but Lockley was able to halt their first attack and Biggins almost played Davison in at the other end. Lewis was pulled up for his first challenge, on Barrow, and given a cautionary word by the referee.

Kelly's free-kick produced danger for Derby as everybody watched Barrow put in his header, but Steele was able to react quickly and turn the ball round for a corner, which Powell cleared.

Wigan were ahead after only five minutes through Newell. A long free-kick from Walsh was headed down and Newell held off the challenge of Streete to plant a cross-shot wide of Steele.

Surprise chance

A lob from Robertson gave

Steve Biggins watches Alex Cribley clear the danger at the Baseball Ground today.

By Gerald Mortimer at the Baseball Ground

DERBY COUNTY: Steele, Palmer, Buckley, Powell, Streete, Lewis, Taylor, Biggins, Davison, Hooks, Robertson. Sub: Pratley.
WIGAN ATHLETIC: Tunks, Cribley, Butler, Kelly, Walsh, Methven, Lowe, Barrow, Johnson, Newell, Langley. Sub: Knowles.
Referee: I. J. Borrett (Harleston).

The half began with a thrilling run by Palmer and although his first centre was blocked, he was able to chip the ball beyond the far post. Robertson tried to volley it and miscued, but Lewis had a low shot scrambled away.

Lewis robbed Butler with a tremendous tackle, but when Powell chipped the ball through, the offside flag was up.

A long free-kick from Kelly the referee, not having a happy time, decided on a goal-kick.

A great cross by Palmer produced a chance at the far post for Biggins, who completely fluffed it and brought the wrath of the crowd down upon his head. He was having a terrible time and was no doubt acutely aware of it.

Davison pulled a goal back after 76 minutes. Streete pushed the ball through and althou[gh]

Mickey didn't score often. But when he did, they were often seriously good goals, and cause for much celebration.

As just mentioned, and as clear from the accuracy of this particular shot, Mickey didn't score very often.

Mickey moved from Derby to Oxford in 1988, in a swap with Trevor Hebberd. Thanks to a rare combination of combative midfield performances and off-pitch dedication, Mickey was soon a cult hero at the Manor Ground.

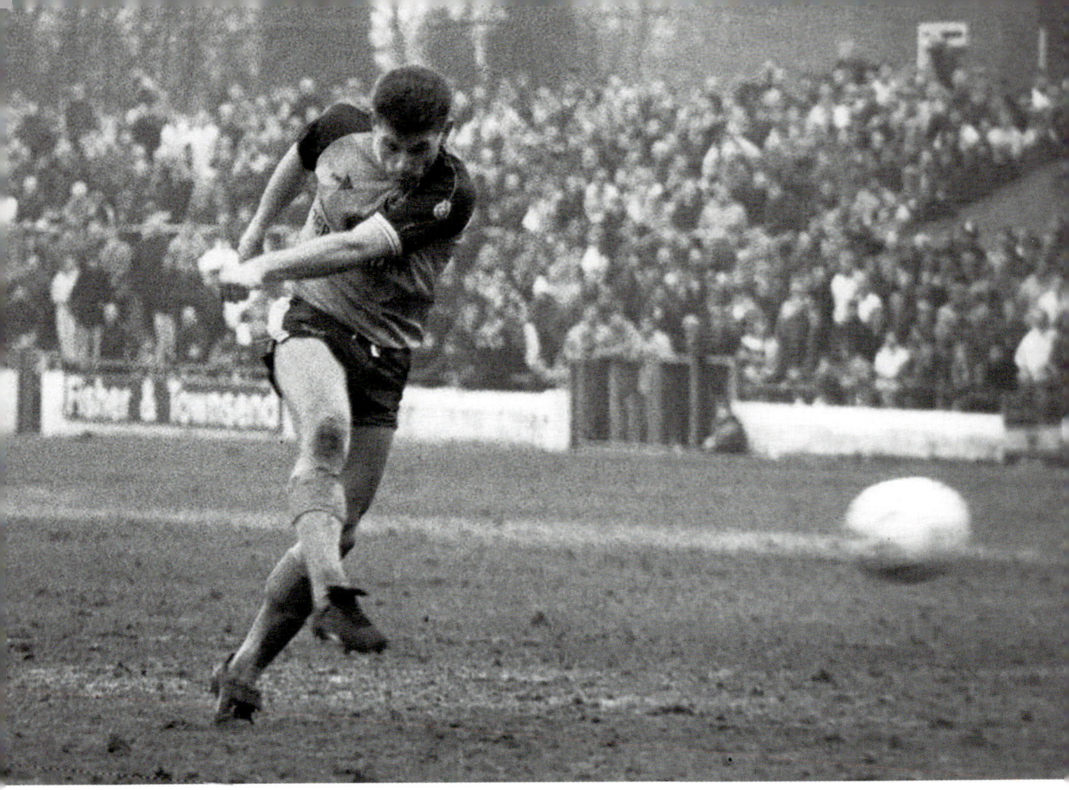

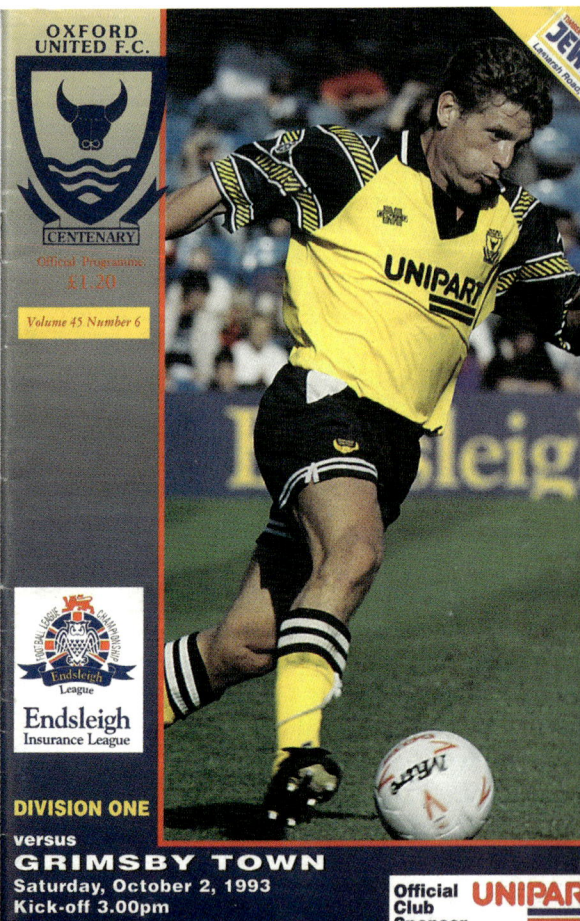

Goal scorer or not, he never tired of shooting. He rarely scored – only netting a handful of times in 400 games – but when he did, they were usually memorable goals.

By the early 1990s, Mickey had established himself as a cult hero at Oxford United. This programme cover captures a typically all-action display in the centre of the Yellows midfield.

OXFORD UNITED F.C.

CENTENARY

Official Programme
£1.20

Volume 45 Number 6

Endsleigh
Insurance League

DIVISION ONE
versus
GRIMSBY TOWN
Saturday, October 2, 1993
Kick-off 3.00pm

Official
Club
Sponsor

UNIPART

Chapter 11

Return of the Mick

IN 2007, with Mickey aged 42 and Doncaster well behind him, his perseverance was rewarded again.

In something of a full circle moment, Mickey returned to his beloved Oxford United to coach the club's youth team. Or that was the original plan, at least.

The club was not in good shape. While Mickey had been away, Firoz Kassam had sold the club. Worse, Oxford had fallen out of the Football League entirely and had been hit hard financially as a result.

Things had turned so sour, in fact, that on the *Oxford Mail* back page announcing Mickey's return to the club's coaching set-up, there is a primer of an article inside the paper in which journalist Jon Murray reflects on 'where it went wrong for Oxford United'. Another back page article reflects on forthcoming wage cuts across the squad, as a portent of the further financial trouble to come.

By the time Darren Patterson was at the club's helm and working to steer the side back into the fourth tier – the lowest division of the fully professional game at the time – he promoted Mickey to become his number two. As he did so, he reminded the local press of Mickey's stature, after his spell away from the club. 'I don't use the word legend lightly, but Mickey is an Oxford United legend.'

Of course, as was typical across the duration of Mickey's association with the club, a managerial change was not far away. And by December 2008, Patterson was out. Chris Wilder, who had just been on the staff at Bury, was appointed to Oxford United's top job.

Wilder described the time himself:

'It happened at The Belfry [golf course]. They asked me if I was interested in getting back into management. I think I was recommended by Alan Hutchinson. Whilst I was at Halifax, we'd have some really tight games against Oxford. And there was the massive Sheffield connection with [former United manager and club director] Jim Smith. I think they were basically impressed with some of the work I'd done, on quite limited resources.'

So, the task ahead for Wilder – getting Oxford United back into the professional and increasingly monied Football League – was huge. The likelihood of success diminished with every year of failure, as the financial gap grew.

It's in these moments where a new manager is not so familiar with the local culture, the history of the club and the expectations of the fans that they often rely on their network to help them make the smartest decisions.

'[Oxford's management] were quite keen for me to dismiss everybody and bring my own people in, but I wanted to know and explore what the present staff were about,' Wilder recalled.

For Wilder, having someone who knew the structure of the club and someone who could help endear him to an increasingly anxious and frustrated fanbase, would be an immense help. Naturally, Mickey's name quickly entered the conversation as a possible candidate.

Dave Penney remembers being on the other side of Wilder's process. 'Chris called me up and said "Mickey Lewis, what do you think?" I just said, "Chris, you can trust him with your life."'

An honest and direct man, Penney is not the type to throw around references like that for fun. Although perhaps he felt slightly indebted to Mickey, having turned up late to his wedding as the best man.

But Penney wasn't the only one to give a stellar recommendation. Wilder told us that after speaking to several other friends and contacts in the game, what came back was universal: 'Selfless, a great guy, incredible work ethic, just so obvious how much he loved the football club.'

It was a full complement of ringing endorsements. And so, Wilder soon decided that Mickey would be 'an ideal foil as number two'.

Incidentally, Wilder described himself in a 2009 *Oxford Mail* piece as 'honest, loyal, *selfish*, obsessive, a bit of a nutter'.

His words, not ours, but it gives us a clue as to why someone like Mickey appealed to him so much. And perhaps it gives a clue as to why Mickey didn't end up as a Premier League number one. More on that later.

* * *

Wilder and Mickey's relationship developed quickly and successfully. A classic good cop, bad cop one-two. And as far as Wilder remembers, Mickey was integral to the club's upturn in fortunes. 'Nobody set the temperature like Mickey,' he said. 'You've got to remember it's not a holiday camp but you're not stuck in a prison.'

Those who worked with Mickey during that time remember a man who understood the game and the club deeply, and who took seriously his responsibility to prepare the team.

He never had an issue telling someone they weren't training properly or digging them out for a lukewarm session. But his overriding instinct was to understand why and what could be done to reverse the situation.

A common Mickey question to one of his players was: 'What's going on, son?' He would know sooner than most when a player was not himself and always had the inclination to seek out that player and offer him support, even if that meant a five-minute chat after training. He was more emotionally in tune with his players than was the norm during that era. He was, in many respects, ahead of his time.

Oxford captain and striker James Constable explained what this approach looked like in practice.

Constable signed slightly before Wilder arrived at the club, making the move away from a Shrewsbury side that was building its attack around future Norwich City hall-of-famer Grant Holt. He remembers arriving at the club and, despite its relatively lowly Conference status, being 'instantly blown away by the ways things were being done, a big part of which was Mickey'.

For Constable and for his team-mates, Mickey was the man who they could go to if they weren't feeling so good or if they weren't in the team. 'He'd be honest and open, he'd tell us when we were falling short, but he'd do whatever it took to get someone back in the team, to get us back playing well.'

And Constable remembers one period in particular, in which he was out of goalscoring form. Mickey took it upon himself to keep taking Constable out on to the grass after training with a bag of balls and an academy goalkeeper. He went further, too, presenting him with a DVD of most of his Oxford goals to help him break out of the negative mindset he had found settling in. Naturally, Constable scored on the Saturday after receiving and watching the DVD.

So, put simply, Mickey quickly proved beyond doubt, in his work with Wilder, that he was a gifted first-team coach-cum-assistant manager. He walked the tightrope between being on the staff but being a friend to the players and he more or less always walked it right.

And Wilder and Mickey soon delivered results.

Wilder's first full season in charge started in ideal fashion. By mid-season, Oxford topped the Conference by five points with a game in hand. Stevenage did ultimately spoil the automatic promotion party, but a win against Rushden & Diamonds set up a play-off final against York City.

What followed was what many suggested was Mickey's favourite day in football.

Chapter 12

Wembley. Or fucking hell, what a weekend

'One of the things that attracted me to Mick, we played hard and we partied hard afterwards. We played to win and if we did, we'd enjoy that. That's so important when you're in the game, a competitive game, that you enjoy it. And we certainly did.'

Chris Wilder, manager of Sheffield United, Northampton Town and Oxford United

MICKEY WAS never one to get unduly exercised by either the ups or the downs of the sport he loved. It was one of the skills that made him such a consistent midfielder and then an effective coach, particularly of young players.

But Wembley is always different, right?

And in May 2010, not long after Mickey's 45th birthday, Oxford United would face York City in the Conference play-off final. And this one meant more than perhaps any other game in Mickey's career.

The new Wembley might not have the history or architectural charm of the old stadium and those famous towers. But it's still the most famous stadium in world football. For national sides, clubs and fans up and down the country – in fact, around the world – it is still the final meeting point, the final reckoning for all of football's hopes and dreams. It is so often the gateway to great riches, as internationals become legends and clubs take one step closer to the Premier League or cement their place in the promised land itself.

The stakes could not have been higher for Oxford. Whilst this was not exactly the Championship play-off final – now infamously billed as the most lucrative game in world football, standing as it does on the precipice of Premier League riches – the game certainly had the potential to be transformational. In fact, back in 2010, as they worked to escape the pain of playing in the fifth tier of English football, Oxford's visit to Wembley felt not far from existential.

The club were languishing. They were too big for England's fifth division. They were too big to be dealing with semi-professional structures and plummeting crowds. But, having been relegated to the Conference at the end of the 2005/06 season, they were no longer newbies in the division. They were at risk of becoming mainstays in the purgatorial world of non-league football, where fans and club staff felt Oxford United surely did not belong.

They'd tried and failed to escape now for the best part of four years. And in the Wembley season itself, they'd spent time at the top of the division before falling out of the automatic promotion places. All of this was happening as the club fell into increasingly significant financial difficulties.

As the long-time sports editor of the *Oxford Mail*, Mark Edwards has watched Oxford United more than most. As he put it: 'It was Oxford's most important day. They went into that knowing that if they failed to win, they'd have been in all sorts of trouble.' In Edwards's words, it was 'quite a dodgy state of affairs'. Oxford legend Jim Smith, who was in a director of football-type job at the time, went on local television to give an interview in which he suggested a loss might spell the end of the club as everyone knew it. The books would only balance for so long.

Wilder recalled all this – particularly that somewhat unhelpful Jim Smith interview – and remembered exactly the pressure this situation created.

'For the Football League teams that drop down to the Conference, there's so much more pressure on them. With Oxford's history, infrastructure and stadium, it was a heavy shirt to wear. And from a financial point of view, the club's future really was on the line. I remember an interview Jim Smith did just before the final. We used to laugh and joke about it. He said if Oxford don't go up, the club's fucked. That was the sort of narrative. The pressure was on.'

In such a heightened situation, it was only natural that the players felt the pressure, too. James Constable, who would captain Oxford at Wembley, put it simply: 'For where we were at, it wasn't going to get much bigger than [the Wembley match].'

So, no big deal then. Just 90 minutes to save a club who were founded in 1893, had tens of thousands of die-hard supporters and only 20 years prior had won the League Cup, one of English football's top prizes.

Yet, despite all the pressure, there was Mickey, in the middle of it all, a picture of calm. The outcome of the match could not have been more important. It might even have had implications for Mickey's longevity at the club if the bleak financial picture painted by Edwards and Wilder was correct. It might even have had implications for Mickey's future in the professional game. But you would never have guessed.

Mickey had been in the dugout for the university Varsity Match between the first and second legs of the semi-final, where, to be frank, the stakes were quite different. Amongst Oxford and Cambridge student players, personal pride, university bragging rights and awards that few outside of those two institutions have heard of or care about were up for grabs. Over at Wembley, where the Varsity Match had not taken place for decades, it was near-existential for an historic club.

But it wasn't like Mickey to make such a distinction. Wherever the pitch and whatever the standard or the stakes, he wanted to win. He wanted to win because he cared about the men and boys in his charge and things mattered to him if they mattered to those around him.

He had said to his wife, Suzanne, that they'd go across to Cambridge, keep quiet, just be there for the boys and then head straight back. He knew he had the second leg of the semi-final just days later. Of course, within seconds of the first whistle, Suzy remembers: 'He was shouting his head off.' And, of course, he headed to the bar after the match, too, to raise a glass with the team.

As one of those in the university camp summed it up: 'Fucking hell, what a weekend.'

* * *

As Mickey turned his attention back to Oxford United and the Wembley final, he seemed as focused on his players and those around the squad – family, friends, staff – as he was the 90-minute challenge ahead of the team in his and Wilder's charge. It was exactly the sort of situation in which he came into his own. He took it upon himself, someone who'd played in his own fair share of big games, in front of enough big crowds, in enough of England's biggest and most famous stadiums, to be the calming influence the Oxford group so clearly needed as they prepared to play in front of 35,000 Oxford fans in what was, for most of them, the biggest game of their lives.

Stalwart of Oxford local radio, Jerome Sale, couldn't help but smile when he remembered exactly how Mickey conducted himself around the match and especially on the advance trip to the stadium, a day or two before kick-off.

The very fact that Sale was there, along with other journalists and media staff like Chris Williams, was itself testament to Mickey's approach. 'The rule was no media,' Williams remembers. 'But Mickey wasn't having it. He snuck us in, basically under the seats, because he knew how much it meant to all of us. He just got people, how they think and feel.'

And Sale particularly recalled a moment from the advance trip that took place on the team bus, as it pulled into the bowels of Wembley. The loading bays underneath the stadium were hives of activity. Not for Oxford United versus York City. Realistically, the FA have and still do schedule such games at Wembley out of a sense of obligation as much as anything else. No, those moving the food and the barrels of beer were most likely clearing out after the FA Cup Final, the culmination of England's most historic and prestigious cup competition, which had taken place the day before.

This part of the journey should have been of little interest to those on the Oxford team coach. That is until the bus got stuck between two concrete pillars as it tried to navigate its way through the people and pallets in its path.

There was a pause. A pop.

One of the bus's windows had fallen straight out of its frame and on to the players sitting below. Fortunately, it hadn't shattered. There was another pause. Then there was a loud voice, from somewhere up at the front of the bus. The voice was unmistakably Mickey's. 'Oi, what's the problem? You could get a bus through there!' The bus erupted with laughter.

By the time that same bus was driving the squad back up the M40 to Oxford, the window still blown through, the atmosphere was such that one might have forgotten all about the match just a day away.

* * *

As much as he was able to relieve pressure and focus on caring for his players on a personal as much as a sporting level, come matchday, Mickey wanted to win as much as anyone at Wembley.

His competitive edge was evident well before the first whistle. He knew Oxford's 35,000-strong crowd would dwarf York's attendance. Pre-match sales figures suggested York would have barely 10,000 in their end. So, as the start of the match edged closer and the time came for the warm-ups to start, Mickey held the players back. He let the York players head out on to the pitch – a pitch they hadn't yet seen, having not made their own advance trip – and then sent the Oxford players running out after them. Mickey knew, of course, the noise with which they'd be greeted. He was long enough in the tooth and had played enough football of his own to know that noise would, in Jerome Sale's words, 'put it up [the York players]'.

The attendance was more or less as the pre-match sales figures had suggested, with a record-breaking 43,000 roaring the two teams out of the tunnel as the match drew closer. Oxford in yellow, York in a red and blue half-and-half. The rain drove down as referee Michael Naylor oversaw the final formalities. Perhaps aided by the lashing rain and a dark, thunderous sky, the sense of the stakes were as palpable for everyone, whether inside the stadium or those watching at home on television. Of course, as the live broadcast of the match cut to the Oxford dugout, Mickey looked as relaxed as ever.

The match itself was frenetic and low on quality. Play-off finals often are and this one was played in challenging wet conditions. But for Oxford, things were soon progressing perfectly. Early goals from Matthew Green and captain James Constable settled the nerves.

But just before half-time, in keeping with a curse that seems to affect many goalkeepers on their big days at Wembley, Ryan Clarke spilled one into his net under little, if any, pressure.

Usually so alive with the buzz of conversation and big match excitement, Edwards remembers the press box almost motionless, totally silent. Four years of non-league football had already been too long for a club that had been routinely visiting the greatest grounds in the country decades before.

From there, the rest of the match was typical of Wembley finals. Stretched, frenetic and stressful. York had their share of chances, with Neil Barrett poking a shot over the bar and substitute Courtney Pitt firing a header that a nervous Ryan Clarke just about scrambled off the line.

United should have sealed it in the 85th minute when Constable blazed over from ten yards out. But, just as the Oxford fans were about to run out of nails to bite, Alfie Potter broke free after a York corner, drilling in a finish to cap off a move that, in truth, was far higher quality than the match that had preceded it.

The final whistle blew, bringing with it a heady mix of euphoria and relief for all those in yellow at the stadium or back in pubs and front rooms across Oxfordshire. Hundreds of Oxford fans swarmed the pitch like fans do on such occasions. There were Mickey and Wilder in the middle of it all, with their coaching colleagues and chairman Kelvin Thomas, posing for a photograph, arms aloft, cheering in jubilant celebration. It's more than just a celebration photo. As Constable put it: 'The pressure of that season, being top, then being back in the play-offs, there was immense pride but also relief.' It is, for Kelvin Thomas, his 'favourite photo in football'.

* * *

Mickey burst into the players' bar soon after the final whistle. He immediately spotted Suzanne and made a beeline straight to her, across the room filled with players, friends and family from both Oxford and York. As Suzanne tells it: 'Mick just came straight through and gave me the biggest hug ever and he never did that, not in those sorts of situations. So, I remember thinking "You're really happy."'

As a diehard Oxford United fan who was as emotional as anyone in the stadium that day, Jim Rosenthal was first to step into the role of master of ceremonies. He'd booked a room at a hotel near to the stadium for the immediate post-match celebrations. He was quick to tell us he's not usually one for being the last man standing at the bar. But he knew as well as anyone the importance of what his beloved team had just achieved and he took seriously the need to toast the heroes of the day. So, let's just say he wasn't going to be driving home once the singing had stopped.

It was chairman Kelvin Thomas who took over the reins as Rosenthal did eventually tap out. As he remembers it, which we have to assume is at least partially accurate, cars were left at Wembley and, whilst the players headed into central London, the staff jumped on the bus and headed straight for Kelvin's favourite pub in Woodstock.

Well, *most* of the players headed to central London. Captain and goalscorer Constable and Mark Creighton – Oxford's defensive enforcer known as 'The Beast' – had both played at Wembley for Kidderminster a couple of seasons prior and remembered all too painfully how they'd packed their shirts and jeans, planning a night out, but then lost that game and taken their unworn clubbing outfits home with them. So, as Oxford's big Wembley day rolled round, the pair had quietly agreed that they weren't about to make the same mistake again.

That did, of course, leave them both stranded as their team-mates reached into their kit bags for the aftershave and proper clubbing attire following the final whistle. London clubs having strict dress code policies, Constable and Creighton were left behind in their tracksuits on the staff coach back to Woodstock. Constable doesn't regret it for a second though: 'It was a fantastic night.'

Naturally, the celebrations stretched deep into the following morning. And when Wilder thinks back to the time, he sees Mickey right there at the heart of it all. 'He was so smart, funny and popular. He always was. To be around people like that, at such a great time, it doesn't get better.'

By the time Sky Sports were arriving in Oxford the next day to interview Kelvin Thomas and Jim Smith, exactly where the play-off trophy could be found became a hotly and urgently debated question. Cue widespread amusement as Thomas and Co. got word that the cup was in bed with Mickey. He had fallen asleep with it next to him after he'd called his mum at 4am.

Despite the late night and surely sore heads, there was little time for rest. Thomas soon summoned the most dedicated revellers back into Woodstock. Several people we spoke to wondered aloud just how many bottles of champagne Thomas bought that day. One went as far as to suggest he's probably still paying off that tab.

* * *

All that was left after that day in Woodstock was the open-top bus tour through Oxford.

The route took the squad and assorted hangers-on from the stadium on the outskirts of the city, down Oxford's Cowley Road and then through the cobbled central streets. Chris Williams, then of the United communications team, remembers a crowd of people being at the stadium to wave the bus off and then, as the bus progressed on its journey, a sea of yellow. Mickey most likely knew or had played in front of most of the people lining the streets. That would surely have been an incredible, career-high feeling, given his history with the club and with the area.

The bus, though, was a sightseeing bus. The sort Oxford has ready-made for the flocks of tourists keen to see where Harry Potter was filmed, the Bridge of Sighs and the Radcliffe Camera. But the thing with those buses is that they don't have any toilets. Williams put it bluntly: 'Everyone had been drinking for three days solid. It was grim.'

At one point, Alfie Potter, who had scored at Wembley, got off the bus, unwilling to relieve himself in a bottle like the majority of his team-mates and the staff. The next thing Williams remembers is Potter chasing down the bus, riding on the handlebars of a fan's bike and Mickey there, hanging over the back of the bus, screaming at the fan to 'go faster, go faster'. And when Mickey wasn't rescuing Potter and hauling him over the edge of the bus, he was making sure Alan Hodgkinson, the goalkeeping coach in his mid-70s, was right there at the front, getting his moment in the sun in front of the yellow sea.

There are some neat parallels between this moment back in 2010 with the more recent bus parade through Oxford, to commemorate the side's 2024 Wembley win in the League One play-off final, which marked their return to England's second tier.

Mickey's son, Zach, was on the bus, ensuring the Lewis family was represented again 14 years after the last city-wide celebration.

And if you look for Zach in the photos of that 2024 parade, it's not so different from looking for Mickey in all the photos from 2010. They're both right there in the middle, arms around another player, cracking a joke or laughing at one themselves. Exactly as you'd expect them to be.

Chapter 13

Eras end

SO, OXFORD United were back in the Football League. The agonising four-year wait was over.

If the fans had come to adore Mickey as a player, his stature at the club had only grown further thanks to his role alongside Wilder in delivering the Wembley win.

Oxford United diehard Shaun Rice told of meeting Mickey in an old bar just a few hundred metres from the training ground. Rice wouldn't have been the only one to catch Mickey an hour or two after training midway through a pint. Rice remembers 'feeling really odd. He was one of my favourite players. I didn't really know what to say.'

Another fan, going by the moniker 'RyanioBirdio' on an Oxford United forum, remembers seeing Mickey walk into the main office at the Kassam. Chris Williams turned to him and said, 'You see that limp? That man gave his leg to our football club.' 'Birdio' added: 'The word legend simply doesn't do him justice.'

However, as it does in football, attention soon turned to the following season. The club were moving in the right direction again, towards the sort of position in the pyramid that the fans felt appropriate for a club like Oxford United. And within the club, minds were focused on ensuring Oxford pulled away as quickly as possible from the dark days of the non-league stay.

The 2010/11 pre-season schedule demonstrated this renewed seriousness, with games against Leicester City and a Manchester United XI.

And in a 24-page *Oxford Mail* supplement printed on the eve of the first match of that 2010/11 season, Wilder urged his players to raise their standards, chairman Kelvin Thomas warned against over-confidence and Mickey laid out a typically direct blueprint for the team and the season: big centre-halves, more mobile forward players and some dry powder for reinforcements in January.

The season itself ended with Oxford comfortably securing a mid-table finish, although there should be no misunderstanding of Wilder and Mickey's ambitions. Wilder noted in a post-season press conference that: 'People will always say that Oxford United have just come up from the Conference, they're tenth in the league, what a good season that is. But for us, it's not good enough.'

So, whilst the following season, 2011/12, was solid again, it was ultimately disappointing, as Oxford dropped out of the play-off spot they'd been occupying for most of the season in the dying throes of the campaign.

The close season then brought with it change. Change that would soon prove consequential for both Wilder and Mickey. Close friend and chairman Kelvin Thomas stepped down after four years at the club, confirming as he did so that he'd be replaced in his role by the club's owner, Ian Lenagan, who would take on the dual owner-chairman role.

It was, for Thomas, who had overseen the escape from the Conference and worked hard to stabilise the club's financial position, the right time to move on to a new challenge. And Lenagan immediately announced his ambition. 'The aim is to leave League Two behind us,' he told the local press. He continued along the same lines:

> 'Chris Wilder and I are both clear about that and the players are clear about that. It won't be easy but if we all pull together, get our heads down and work hard, we can achieve the ambition that the players, the staff and the supporters all share. Promotion.'

But despite this statement of ambition, the 2012/13 season was another story of Wilder and Mickey not quite being able to secure the promotion the club and fans were so desperately chasing.

* * *

Finances were a particular problem. Despite Lenagan's statements of ambition, it was clear there was nowhere near enough money to mount a serious tilt towards the division above and beyond. The team would often have four- or five-hour journeys home after games because the club couldn't afford overnight stays. There were several personal disputes between players and the club. Some staff claimed they weren't being paid on time.

There were also changes in the mood around the club and in the boardroom – with the likes of Kelvin Thomas and Jim Rosenthal no longer associated with the club – that left Wilder feeling as though the time was right for change.

And so it was that things grew increasingly difficult for Wilder as the club continued to plug away in League Two. His relationship with the board – and at times with the fans – grew increasingly frayed. For Jerome Sale, 'it just got a bit weird'. As Thomas put it: 'Chris needed to get out.'

In late January 2014, Wilder decided to leave the club. He would be moving to Northampton Town. At first glance, it might have seemed an unexpected and unusual move. Wilder would be shifting from a team that had re-established its Football League credentials to relegation candidates who were facing a return to the abyss that Wilder had recently been fighting so hard to escape. Of course, history would ultimately see it differently. After two years under Wilder, the Cobblers made it to League One with a division record 99 points. The team they pipped? Oxford United, who suddenly seemed as trapped in League Two as they had been in the division below.

We don't know exactly how Mickey fitted into Wilder's plans at that moment. Paul Lee thought that Wilder might take Mickey with him. James Constable recalls the two men being joined at the hip and it being a surprise that Mickey didn't make the move. But Wilder himself remembers the time a little differently.

Just as he needed a fresh start at Northampton, he felt that he probably needed a new voice beside him. Wilder found this in the highly regarded Alan Knill, who quickly became Wilder's new right-hand man and then stayed there. Dan Bond wondered if 'Chris didn't think Mickey's coaching was that state of the art.' Wilder, though, rejected this notion: 'Leaving without Mickey was certainly no slight on his ability.'

As time passes and memories inevitably change and fade, there is clearly a lot of conjecture, rather than concrete evidence, as to the situation at the time. But one thing that is certain is that Wilder's departure created an opportunity for Mickey to begin his second stint in caretaker charge of the team.

Just as it had done the first time, the move made perfect sense – for all parties, inside and outside the club. New executive chairman Ian Lenagan was acutely aware of the merits of giving Mickey a chance at the top job. And he was soon commenting to the *Oxford Mail* that he was impressed by the buzz Mickey created at the training ground: 'Everybody noticed it.' Andy Whing was a member of the squad at the time and he remembers being 'more delighted for him than for myself that we won'. This sense of positivity was quickly flowing through the fanbase, too. A fanbase that, by this point, revered him.

Lifelong fan Phil Chambers had grown up watching Mickey from the Manor Ground terraces and he remembers seeing Mickey soon after his appointment. Nervous about the consequences of a downturn in results, he asked him to promise to get the squad going again. 'Aye, we'll be fine,' Mickey replied.

Just like everyone else associated with the club, Matthews wanted nothing more than for that to be true.

Why? Because they knew Mickey was one of them, wanting to win just as much as they did. How could they think otherwise? Across what by this point was nearly three decades, he'd done pretty much every job at the club, from driving the minibuses to playing central midfield.

He was loyal in an industry that, increasingly, didn't do loyalty. There were 13 managerial changes in the 2013/14 Premier League season – part of a trend that was beginning to make its way through the English Football League, too, as the financial stakes grew higher and boards and fans alike became increasingly impatient.

But while Lenagan initially left open the door to making Mickey's appointment permanent – downplaying external interest in the job by pointing out that 'United need the right person, not the right name' – Mickey's caretaker spell simply didn't go as well as hoped.

As too many club boards have found out, appointing a legend doesn't always lead to the success they hoped for. Just ask whoever hired Frank Lampard, twice, or Ole Gunnar Solskjær. And despite Mickey's best efforts, the team was soon nosediving. In Chris Williams's words: 'He just didn't pick up the points he needed to.'

Exactly why this happened is one of those questions in football that will never have a simple answer. Mickey was obviously inheriting the same dire financial situation that had led to Wilder's departure. The squad was the same, too. So, there was likely only so much he could do and there's only so much that can change based on charisma alone.

Striker and Wembley hero James Constable also struggled for a neat explanation. 'It was so frustrating. Results just started to slip. We had more than enough in that changing room. We felt like we let Mickey and the staff down.'

By March 2014 – a year before Mickey's 50th birthday – his time as caretaker manager was over. He was to become assistant manager to the newly appointed Gary Waddock.

When Michael Appleton took over from Waddock shortly after that, and following nearly three decades of association with the club, Oxford United asked Mickey Lewis to leave for the final time.

* * *

It is interesting to consider why Mickey was not asked, or perhaps didn't push as hard as he could have, to join Wilder. Particularly as Wilder was soon on an ascent to the very top of English football with Sheffield United. Was Mickey ruthless enough? Did he want to commit everything, at the expense of his family, to football? Could he, even if he had wanted to? We will explore these questions later.

We can focus on certainties for now. As Michael Appleton came in to take the Oxford United top job full-time in the summer of 2015, Mickey was on his way out of the club in what the *Oxford Mail* reported as being a 'significant change' to the first-team coaching staff.

And this time, it was final.

Mickey likely thought that his record of service meant he was deserving of much greater clarity. The final decision to ask him to leave the club was made late into the summer, limiting his ability to go and find new work in time for the new season, against the backdrop of the mortgage he and Suzanne had just taken out on a house in Oxford. A house they had just moved into with their young son, Zach.

But none of this seemed to matter to the powers that be. Some of those who were there at the time recalled a sense from the new leadership that the club wasn't moving forward as it should have been doing and that it was time for a clean sweep. There was a feeling in some quarters, according to one club employee, that 'the old regime had to go'.

* * *

There is no hiding that this part of Mickey's story, as he left the club with which he'd been associated since his early 20s, in difficult circumstances, was one of the hardest moments of his career. And friends and colleagues of Mickey's have helped us to try and understand how Mickey processed all this tumult.

As Chris Williams saw it:

'He was a bit heartbroken the second time. It hurt him, hurt his pride. When he ended up at Oxford City, we'd go and see him, he'd be coaching, and he'd always say "Stop. I need to go and talk to Mr Williams." He wanted to connect, always, just to hear the latest goings-on, not because he wanted to control anything, but because he just loved the club so much.'

But he was also never going to be one to let this moment derail him. He had been around football long enough to know how the business worked. And sulking wasn't really in his nature. As Kelvin Thomas put it: 'He was never the type to be down for long. He always came back jovial, making light of events. I think it came down to the fact he understood his responsibility to Suzanne and Zach. It also would never have affected his friendships.'

And that, really, was Mickey. He was a man who moved forward and moved on. He was probably acutely aware that the pathway to coaching or managing at the top of the game was now looking incredibly challenging, if not impossible. But what Mickey soon found instead was something very different. He found something earthier, more grassroots, more in touch with the sort of footballers and the sort of football that had shaped him as a teenager back in Birmingham all those years prior. He found an environment similar to the one that had produced the 'bolshie Brummie' who got booked after two minutes at Selhurst Park on his debut in December 1981.

And, frankly, Oxford United's loss was others' gain. Without this unforeseen and admittedly unwanted fork in the road, Mickey may have stuck it out on the bruising treadmill of the professional game. Had he done so, many of the people mentioned in the pages that follow, and particularly many young people, may have missed out on the education of a lifetime.

Chapter 14

'Shit in her fuckin' handbag'

HAVING LEFT Oxford United in 2015, for the final time and in somewhat acrimonious circumstances, Mickey might have been tempted to take some time away from the dressing room to lick his wounds. Or, at the very least, he might have shown signs that his love for the sport that was knocking him back with increasing frequency was slowly diminishing.

But again, that just wasn't Mickey.

In addition to continuing with his duties at the university, he was soon building another roster of roles. That roster took him to Reading academy and Oxford City's Velocity youth programmes. He also picked up new work in some unlikely places, not least at Eton College.

He also soon linked up with Tristan Lewis at Hayes & Yeading, a semi-professional club that was playing in the seventh tier of English football, the Southern League. By the time he was bringing Mickey to the club, Tristan had transitioned from the Hayes & Yeading dugout to become the club's director of football.

Now, football is always a tough business. But non-league football is extraordinarily tough and life at Hayes was even tougher still. When Tristan hired Mickey, the club had £1,800 in the bank. The job Mickey was taking on meant late nights, handfuls of fans and working out how to hire Hayes' own stadium, because the money given to the club by Hillingdon Council had frittered away.

The manager's office was a portacabin. When they weren't out on the pitch, Tristan and Mickey would often be in that cabin trying to construct something that looked at least a little like a competitive team.

All of this should have made for a miserable experience. It was closer to Des Moines Menace than it was to Wembley. It was closer to Des Moines Menace than it was the Premier League. A league that, by this point, Chris Wilder was hurtling towards with Sheffield United. On some days, it surely was as miserable as it sounds.

But when we asked Tristan how he felt about that era of 'no budget, very average players and a shit ground', he said it was enjoyable. Because of Mickey.

In fact, Tristan remembers fondly a time in which Mickey's love for football burned as brightly as ever and a time in which his passion for developing young players came to the fore, perhaps more strongly than it had ever done before.

There was the afternoon in the portacabin when the pair tried to seal a deal for one of the players who, presumably with few other options, seemed open to joining the club.

'We were trying to strengthen the team. And this lad has agreed to come. He bought into what we were trying to do. And he asks about a signing fee. Mick was just like, "Are you fucking joking? When I signed my first deal, do you know how much I got? The manager turned around and gave me a sweatshirt. My signing-on fee was a fucking jumper." And so, of course, Mickey then turned round and picked up a jumper that was lying around, gave it to the lad and told him the deal was done. Which it was.'

And there were several all-time classic examples of Mickey's rare ability to command difficult or despondent changing rooms, and to defuse changing-room tension, too.

While a player was talking over Mickey's pre-match tactical advice, Mickey turned to him and asked: 'Sorry mate, but am I a cunt?' The player quickly got the message and started to listen.

But that is not the team talk that Tristan *really* remembers.

To set the scene: a club in decline, a management team overworked and a side in terrible form, having lost five on the bounce. The records even state that Hayes & Yeading's attendance at Beaconsfield Road at the time of the team talk in question was zero.

False information, surely, but a lack of any reliable record has got to say something about the state of affairs in this oft-overlooked grey outpost in west London.

By necessity, as much as Mickey's preference, Hayes had a young team and the situation, coupled with the poor form, meant confidence was fragile and the mood was low.

So, in search perhaps of a different angle from which to motivate his motley crew of young, down-on-their-luck non-leaguers in desperate need of inspiration, Mickey strode into the changing room to deliver his pre-match remarks.

'Right lads, come on. What's this all about?'

Tristan couldn't help but laugh as he told the story.

'I want you to imagine we're in a nightclub.'

Some quizzical looks.

'You're not the best-looking lad in this place. None of you are the best-looking lads. We know we're struggling.'

Some of the players start to shift in their seats.

'We've had a little bit of eyes with a girl all night. We think we're on to one. It's getting late, you're about to get kicked out.'

The lads are still unsure, but a little more confident that they're in for a great pay-off.

'And then, just like that, she's fucked off with someone else.'

Now they're in. Studs are thudding the floor. Some of the lads are stood up. Grins widen. The girl we've been eyeing all night? Fucked off with someone else?

What do you want us to do? We'll do whatever you say, gaffer.

'I want you to pick her handbag up.'

Alright. We will. We'll pick her fucking handbag up. What shall we do with it?

'And shit in it.'

Excuse me?

'That's right, lads. The opposition today, they're the girl that's fucked off with someone else. And I want you to go out there today, I want you to get their handbag and shit in their fuckin' handbag!'

The backroom staff stare at Mickey in amazement. Did he actually just say that? Then comes the roaring, stomach-buckling, time-stopping laughter.

And so it was, in that moment, that no one remembered they hadn't won in weeks. No one cared that they were playing in an empty stadium the club didn't even own.

Mickey had once again shown his ability to manipulate a situation so that no one ever doubted themselves. So that people remembered why they played football, even in situations where the stakes were high and luck was low.

Would an Amazon *All or Nothing* docuseries of that Hayes & Yeading season have led to Mickey getting cancelled on social media? Perhaps. But this was a coach and a man-manager who would try just about anything to get a smile out of his players, to keep a head from dropping, to keep a team, a club and a fanbase going. For another half, another game, another season.

No surprises, then, that Hayes & Yeading have named an award after him. It's not for the best footballer, but instead for the best person. Because Mickey was exactly that and someone who brought the best out of others, too. As Tristan put it, as a final reflection on that period: 'I don't know anyone – *anyone* – who has a bad word to say about him.'

He adds: 'In football, that is so, so rare.'

Chapter 15

Goodbye to all that

MICKEY ULTIMATELY left Hayes & Yeading in late 2016, returning to two of his great loves, leading the university side and working with young players in Oxford City's Velocity football and education programme.

The move brought to an end Mickey's time as a coach in the professional and semi-professional game.

But in doing so the move also creates a vantage point from which to look back across the journey that took him from the West Brom academy and England youth tournaments in Europe to becoming Oxford United's 'Mad Dog', which was a period in which he enjoyed a triumphant visit to Wembley with the club and city he came to love and call home.

Whether he was crashing into a tackle at The Hawthorns, calming his players at Wembley or putting his arm around a youngster at Oxford City who just needed a friend, he gave everything he had to the people around him and to the clubs for which he worked. He guaranteed a performance.

Ross Weatherstone reflected emotionally on a relationship with Mickey that had started on the terraces of the Manor Ground and stretched through Oxford United's youth and senior teams and, truthfully, through much of Weatherstone's life. He recalled that Mickey would 'always say "The game owes you nothing, you owe it everything, give it your all." And you know, he gave everything. And he never wanted anything in return.'

And Jim Magilton captured the impact this quality of Mickey's had on everyone around him: 'The one thing you want to give people is enthusiasm every day to want to be better. Mickey did that. Every single day of his career, on the pitch and in the dugout.'

But Mickey knew better than anyone that, while you can guarantee a performance, you can never guarantee a result. And the results didn't always follow. And so, in many ways, his experience at the end of his career and particularly at Hayes exemplifies a broader point.

At no point of Mickey's playing or coaching career did he ascend to the very top of the game. He was a highly competent, competitive midfielder near the top of the English football pyramid. That is no mean feat and it is far more than most others with footballing ambitions have ever achieved. But even at the peak of his powers, he was never going to interest Manchester United or trouble the outer reaches of an England senior squad.

The same pattern can be seen in his long and winding coaching career, during which he spent as much time working with amateur footballers as he did top-level professionals.

But at Hayes, as it was across his career, he achieved an outsized impact that stretched far, far beyond any three-point win, individual glory or promotion campaign. That was particularly true in how Mickey was able to influence the youngsters he played with and coached, as they embarked on their own footballing and personal journeys. Journeys to becoming better players but also better men. And journeys which, during our time playing for Mickey as university footballers, we both experienced first-hand.

So just how was it that Mickey was able to reach beyond the limitations of his own career to achieve a deep and lasting imprint on so many, including so many of those who were at the Kassam for his memorial in October 2021? What exactly was it about him that secured a legacy far greater and deeper than many of those who did make it to the top of English football, into national squads or to managerial glory?

That is where we go next.

SECTION TWO:

DON'T LET IT PASS YOU BY

Chapter 16

Tough at the top

'What came across most of all was his care for young players. The way he spoke about them as though they were his own children, his own family. He wanted them to do well and to get well educated. I learned from him. I wanted to be like that.'

Martin Allen, Queens Park Rangers and West Ham United midfielder, long-serving English football manager

'I remember when I finally scored my first goal. He said, "You'll score loads." Mickey made an effort. That was Mickey. He'll take time for the youngsters. He helped any and everyone.'

Paul Wanless, Oxford United team-mate

MICKEY WAS a real players' coach. Whether he was in charge or working as an assistant, he was always the one the players felt they could go to. The one the players felt had their back. Players generally appreciated his tactical philosophy, similar as it was to his approach as a player: play fast and play hard. And they appreciated the more fundamental view he took of football – and, really, of life – as he regularly reminded those around him: 'Don't let it pass you by.'

And in the time we both spent with Mickey while he coached the University of Oxford first team, it is clear to us that, as much as these talents brought success in the men's professional game, Mickey had a rare and profound gift for coaching and shaping young people.

That was true whether he was responsible for the through-line from Oxford United's academy into the club's first team, overseeing football education programmes across Oxfordshire, taking charge of a squad of enthusiastic (but often limited) amateurs in the Oxford versus Cambridge Varsity Match or introducing the under-eights at his local Sunday league side, the Stonesfield Strikers, to the offside rule for the first time.

In the section that follows, which dips back into many of the locations and situations we've already introduced, we've tried to understand exactly why that was the case, whilst charting the remarkable impact Mickey had on so many young lives.

* * *

As we seek to understand Mickey's approach to coaching young players, it's important first to understand Mickey's own experience as a young player working to break into the professional game.

Whilst we've already charted Mickey's early breakthrough into the West Brom first team and the impression he quickly left on senior players like Martin Jol, he also played well over 50 games for West Brom's reserves in the long-defunct Central League. It was a time when Mickey surely learnt many of the lessons he would later use when developing his own approach to young players.

Mickey described this time in his life, his mid-teenage years, in an interview with Laurie Rampling, West Brom's photographer and historian. The interview was part of a series of conversations Rampling conducted with those who, at various points, have called West Brom home.

'Straight from joining the club from school as an apprentice, as we called it then, four or five of us youngsters played for the reserves. There was only one substitute back then. The club didn't take 20 players anywhere in those days. You would play on the same day as the first team, then you would play midweek and we used to play with six or seven senior players and we would play against Manchester United and Liverpool.

'When I look at some of the things that go on now, the kids can't get the same experience that we did. We used to play against men when we were 16, against the likes of Liverpool's reserves and they used to put good teams out, not like now when it's under-21s or under-23s. I used to play against players like Jan Molby at Liverpool. You played with first-team players. At

West Brom, you had five or six senior players playing
in your team and that was, for me, a great upbringing.'

So, by the time Mickey was making his league debut for the
Baggies' first team at the age of 16, he had played regularly
at The Hawthorns. He'd played, too, at Anfield and at Old
Trafford.

As Mickey and Rampling talked about young players like
Kemar Roofe, Adil Nabi and George Thorne, Mickey recalled
how the experience that he and his peers had in the 1970s and
1980s was a far cry from the situation today. And whilst nostalgia
and hindsight can so often be uncomfortable bedfellows, in this
case, the change is not necessarily for the better.

'It's tough for kids now at the top level. It's really tough.
But we were lucky. They just used to throw us in. You
were playing regularly in the reserves. So, if there was
an injury, they just used to put you into the team.'

So, Mickey's approach to working with young people is best
understood from this foundational time. A time in which
Mickey and the young players around him were expected to
work hard but were given the opportunities and support to enjoy
themselves and to perform.

* * *

Mickey went on to work with the full spectrum of young
footballers after his playing career.

His first coaching job was in 1996 with the Oxford United youth team and he followed that up with a broad range of work in non-league, in the Reading academy and on programmes in Oxford for boys recently released from academies but with hopes not yet extinguished. In each of these instances, he was responsible for young men and boys desperately striving for one of football's greatest prizes: full admission to the professional game.

At the same time, with the students at places like the University of Oxford and Eton College or with the pre-teens at Stonesfield Strikers, he was coaching players like us. Players with no hope of ever reaching the big time.

But he brought the approach and philosophy he had learned during his days with West Brom, as a youth player playing in the Central League, irrespective of where he was coaching. An approach based on the setting of high expectations, but an emphasis, too, on enjoyment and opportunity. He honed this approach with a skill for communication and an impressive empathy for youngsters.

He prioritised development over results in a way that seems normal now but would have been progressive in the late 90s and early noughties. And he treated everyone he met, worked with and coached the same – with a deep kindness and respect, whether they were a no-hoper or a cocky striker eyeing a professional deal worth thousands of pounds a week.

It was an approach that resonated with and impacted deeply those in his charge. Too many who contributed to this book, including Des Buckingham, described him as a father figure in their lives for it to be a coincidence or cliché.

At the time of writing, Buckingham is Oxford United's manager, overseeing a first season in England's second tier for over 20 years, having masterminded a Wembley play-off final win at the end of the 2023/24 season.

He first met Mickey as a young man trying to make his own way in the professional game, as a player in a local Oxford college programme.

It was an early version of the type of programme that has become much more popular in recent years, picking up young players who haven't made it as scholars at the professional clubs to which they've dedicated so many of their teenage years and attempting to prevent them from falling through the cracks that can, in the circumstances, be so damaging.

Buckingham talked as he reflected on that time about a 'three-year, unbelievable journey' with a group of friends with whom he's still in close touch and still talk often about Mickey.

When that group of friends remember their time at the college, and their time under Mickey's wing, they reflect on the fact that they've 'never met anyone so enthusiastic about delivering a single training session' or 'someone so good at simplifying [the game]' for the players in their charge.

And they're memories that leave Buckingham, one of the most exciting young managers in England today, in no doubt about the impact of Mickey on his life and career.

'[The college programme] was the first time in my life I'd come across someone who was so good at their job. He made me as good a player as I could have been. But it was about the soft skills he used to make me a better man, too. The way he made you feel, the sense of humour, the trust. The way he was able to communicate and get the best out of you.

'In my first ten years of coaching, I genuinely just tried to copy Mick. I loved the way he was able to transmit knowledge and engage. I tried to copy the things that he was doing. When I look back at it now, I'd say a lot of those things have stuck to become my values. Respect, empowerment, collaboration. Those values I've got now are just massively embedded because of him.'

So, as much as Mickey made his name in the professional game as a player and then a coach, he built a lot of his reputation – as well as his legacy – as a coach of young players, particularly in and around Oxfordshire.

So much so that many of those we spoke to, including in the stories that follow now – naturally starting with Mickey's time coaching the youth team at Oxford United, the club at which he spent so much of his career – remember Mickey as one of their favourite coaches.

Many even called him the greatest coach they'd ever had.

Chapter 17

Hunger in paradise?

ROSS WEATHERSTONE was ten when he first watched Mickey Lewis play football.

Standing on the terrace of the old Manor Ground as one of Oxford United's youngest fans, Weatherstone came to love and admire Mickey very quickly, given the way he played the game. As is always so important to fans young and old, Mickey made you think the result mattered as much to him, or even more, than it did to anyone else in the ground.

So, Weatherstone was understandably a little star-struck by the time he was 15 and Mickey was pulling him aside, after a youth team training session at Oxford United, telling him the club wanted him around and that he'd be playing for the youth team that Saturday. The way Weatherstone describes that moment perfectly encapsulates the crux of Mickey's impact as a coach: 'I can't remember the words he said, but I remember the way he made me feel ten feet tall.'

That was a particular knack of Mickey's. He saw those players who were perhaps a little overawed or uncertain in their abilities to play to the level being asked of them. He'd go out of his way to, as Hayes & Yeading player Adam Everitt put it, 'make you feel like a good player'. Craig Adey, who coached with Mickey in Oxford, regularly saw Mickey 'make players feel taller, make players feel faster'.

Weatherstone's youth team debut was against Crystal Palace. His brother, Simon, one of the many young players that Mickey coached who is now working at the very top of the match – at Newcastle, in the Premier League – was starting the game. Ross was on the bench, but the two brothers were swapped in and out around the hour mark. Ross recalled: 'He just appreciated these sorts of things. It pissed my brother off. But in his way of managing people, he said "Look, you guys will remember this for the rest of your lives. Treasure it."' And the brothers do, still talking about that afternoon, 25 years later.

Weatherstone reflected back on that time from his vantage point now as a qualified teacher. 'Mickey had this magical way of doing things, of understanding how and why learning and development happened, and in a way that felt totally personal to you.' He noted, too, that Mickey used to make it mandatory for all the youth team players in his charge to see the club psychologist whenever they were available.

It was this empathy and ability to meet his players as the emotional young people they were that made Mickey so effective – so often, we were told, in partnership with the late Oxford United kitman Ken Ridley, in whom Mickey found a similarly minded friend and drinking partner – and that meant so many people so cherished working with him.

But it went further than that. There was a mutual respect between Mickey and the young players he worked with. This respect was rooted in the humility with which Mickey carried himself. For someone who's had a football career that so many in the country could only dream of, it would have been all too easy for Mickey to talk frequently about all he'd achieved in the game.

For many coaches, playing achievement can quickly become a lazy substitute for coaching merit. But that wasn't Mickey. If his playing career came up, he'd 'um' and 'ah' and say it was a different lifetime. For Weatherstone, he doesn't think he's 'ever met anyone since that carried as much humility as Mick'. None of that is to say Mickey was a pushover.

Weatherstone was, at times, a troublemaker. He remembers a particular journey in the youth team minibus. Inevitably, Mickey was driving. In his teenage boredom and undoubtedly encouraged by his team-mates and friends, Weatherstone sprayed water out of the window at a group of passers-by. Unfortunately for Weatherstone, Mickey saw the incident.

Back at the club Mickey set about punishing the errant youngster. In fact, he made Weatherstone 'wash anything and everything that could be washed at the club'. Boots, balls, buses. The whole lot.

But with Mickey, it was never punishment for punishment's sake. Mickey saw that Weatherstone took his new duties seriously and he continued to train well. So, he pushed him up into the first team within weeks of the minibus incident.

* * *

Weatherstone isn't the only person who remembers Mickey's work with the Oxford United youth players in this way.

Des Buckingham, who also spent time in the Oxford United youth set-up, remembers that whenever the youth team were playing against or training with the first team, it was clear where Mickey's instincts and allegiances lay.

It was in one such game – on a Wednesday, for the first-team squad members who hadn't been involved in a game the night before – that Buckingham saw Mickey lose his cool in a way that he so rarely did.

Carried away by his competitive edge or bruised by his lack of involvement in first-team affairs, one of the senior pros overstepped the mark and hurled a volley of abuse at one of the youngsters. Mickey stopped the game immediately, charging across the pitch towards the senior pro in question. And he left the player in no doubt as to what he'd thought of the misstep: 'If you ever, ever speak to a player like that again, we're going to have a serious problem.'

Mickey's protective nature was there for all to see. And not just when it suited him, in the relative privacy and low stakes environment of a club training ground.

* * *

Banbury United Football Club are a staple of the Oxfordshire non-league football circuit. Over the years, that's made them a perfect pre-season foil for Oxford United's youth teams.

Mickey took a particularly young group over to Banbury's long-time home at Station Approach for one such pre-season occasion.

Few seem to recall the exact make-up of the group or indeed the score on the day. But Neil Crosby dialled in on that particular match in a tribute to Mickey posted on Instagram.

Crosby's post vividly described Banbury's ageing midfield enforcer taking it upon himself to impart some lower-league wisdom on to his youthful opponents.

One can only speculate as to the reasons behind a journeyman non-league bruiser wanting to use this pre-season fitness test as an opportunity to kick a 17-year-old or two. Perhaps he saw something of his own faded and forgotten promise in the pretenders zipping around him. Perhaps it was all he knew.

Either way, Mickey didn't take kindly to the wanton aggression. Of course, Mickey had never shied away from a battle in the middle of the park during his own playing career. But he rightly saw this particular display of physicality as unnecessary and mismatched, unfolding as it did in a men-versus-boys late summer friendly.

Crosby remembers him firing off a couple of warning shots from the away dugout. You can imagine exactly what was said. 'What's the fucking point of that, pal?' 'What the fuck are you trying to prove, mate?' Or words to that effect.

A couple of tackles followed to suggest the warning shots had fallen on deaf ears.

So, there was Mickey, strapping his boots up, finding whatever spare bits of kit he could from the bags littering the dugout around him and winding his knees into gear.

On he went, the next time the ball went out of play. And 30 seconds later, as if he was back chasing after a prime John Barnes, he'd kicked the Banbury enforcer a foot or two into the air. There was no intent to injure, of course, but enough venom to make sure that his point had been made.

Mickey then immediately substituted himself off. His job was done. The youth team could play out the rest of their match in peace.

* * *

There was a remarkable consistency and longevity to Mickey's approach. Despite the setbacks he experienced, whether his first departure from Oxford or his premature exit at Doncaster, he maintained an unerring commitment to youth development throughout his career.

And so it was, some years later, in the early 2010s and during Mickey's final stint at Oxford United, that Dan Bond arrived at the club to join Mickey on Chris Wilder's coaching staff. Fresh out of university, Bond started an internship with the first team, in performance analysis. Bond himself described it as an 'unlikely and unbelievable first job'.

The job was far from straightforward. Bond remembers the club at the time as a daunting place for someone of his age. There were senior players, who Bond chose not to name, who could be 'horrible fuckers if they thought you weren't pulling your weight'. That was perhaps normal for any professional football dressing room at the time – and probably still is now in many places – but he also found it difficult to work with the notoriously demanding Wilder.

He wasn't the only one. The head of sports science for whom Bond had come to work was soon out of the door. This was before the days of a 15- or 20-person first-team staff, so Bond was left on his own as head of his department, essentially without cover or protection. All this combined to create a situation in which Bond was, by his own admission, totally out of his depth.

But, of course, Bond wasn't really left on his own. He wasn't really without cover. This was the sort of situation in which Mickey thrived. He was Bond's calming influence, his arm round the shoulder, the one going out of his way to tell him to relax, to just do the job to the best of his ability. 'If Mickey wasn't there, I'd have been out of there.'

Around the time Bond was benefitting from the protection of Mickey's ever-generous wing, Sam Long was making his way through Oxford United's ranks, with his eyes firmly set on the first team. Long has since served as Oxford's captain and, at the time of writing, he's part of the squad that's enjoying Oxford's return to Championship football under the stewardship of Des Buckingham.

Long, too, was quick to stress how much credit he gives Mickey for the career he's had to date, just like Buckingham was in his own contribution. Long and Mickey's relationship, which Long also described as somewhat paternal, started when Mickey was assistant to Wilder and Long was top boy in United's youth team.

Long has particular memories of the night when he and his dad were travelling to Barnsley for the third round of the prestigious FA Youth Cup, that most prized of competitions for English football's aspirational young bucks. The journey was their third attempt at a match that had already been called off twice for snow.

Mickey had driven up on his own but, thanks to an errant turn or two, had ended up in intense weather-related traffic on the wrong side of the motorway near the ground. Ever committed to watching the club's young players, Mickey abandoned his car on the side of a frosted motorway and hopped across the barriers to jump in with Long and his dad, just to make sure he didn't miss the kick-off. It was typical Mickey. If he had to run across an icy motorway somewhere outside of Barnsley to be on the touchline for a youth game, then so be it.

* * *

By the time Wilder was moving on to Northampton and Mickey had taken caretaker charge in early 2014, the first-team squad was struggling with injuries. A typical Football League test awaited away at Morecambe on a cold, boggy February afternoon.

Long was 19 and couldn't drive, so was travelling up with the squad masseuse, 'Spike'. After a detour to Kwik Fit to deal with Spike's flat tyre, Mickey had his arm round Long and was putting him in the team for the following day's match. He even built the day's set piece strategy around him. 'They won't expect us to aim for Longy. He's our secret weapon.'

It was the sort of pre-match move that would make even a more experienced player feel that little bit taller. Mickey, of course, would have known that, too.

Most will likely remember the game itself as a drab 1-1 in a long-line of hard-fought but ultimately unfruitful draws that Mickey oversaw whilst in caretaker charge of the club for the second time.

Morecambe's Robbie Threlfall scored in the 92nd minute to cancel out an earlier deflected David Connolly strike that had put Oxford ahead. As desperate as so many around Oxford United were to see Mickey succeed and get the job full-time after Wilder's departure, it was more points dropped in the bitter struggle to escape the division.

Mickey was disappointed at the manner of the dropped points and his side's continued slide out of the automatic promotion places. He knew that time was running out to demonstrate his credentials for a longer-term run at the job he wanted so badly.

But even in these unique circumstances where it was his own head on the line, the result once again seemed to quickly fade in significance for Mickey. Instead, he was thinking to phone Long as soon as he could after the match: 'Well played, Longy, keep going son.'

A dreary 1-1 draw, perhaps, but an afternoon and a phone call Long has never forgotten.

Chapter 18

Sliding down the pyramid

SO, MICKEY'S impact on young players was consistently profound across his time associated with Oxford United. But by the time Mickey was in the dugout at Hayes & Yeading in 2016, it might seem fair to assume that he'd been hardened by the industry that had at times been so brutal to him. Mickey's priorities could easily have started shifting towards preserving his own position in the game. Even non-league football was and is, above all, a results business.

Still, though, Mickey's commitment to developing young players remained unerring. Where others might have reverted to the safest possible route to short-term success, Mickey's approach was as it always had been. He remained totally focused on giving opportunities to the people he thought had earned them, irrespective of age.

Andy Whing played for Mickey at Oxford United. He's now building a successful coaching career and at the time of writing is in charge of Solihull Moors in the National League. He knows intimately the pressures on a manager in modern football. 'A lot of managers and experienced coaches, they sometimes don't have the patience with young players. It's such a ruthless industry, everybody wants success now.'

But Whing recalls Mickey had no such problem, even once he'd arrived at Hayes. 'Mickey had a huge amount of patience. He was able to try and develop the lads. The younger players related to him.'

Tristan Lewis was director of football at Hayes when Mickey was appointed as manager and he remembers Mickey just as Whing does. If you read Mickey's first interview after his appointment to the role, you don't have to wait long for him to start talking effusively about the club's youth set-up and his excitement about giving the club's brightest young prospects their first opportunities in the first team and the men's game.

In a more recent interview that Mickey did with Laurie Rampling, back at West Brom, he said the same: 'I said I'd [take the Hayes job] mainly because they had a lot of really good young players.'

And Mickey stayed true to his football philosophy – and, really, his outlook on life – even as results went against him at Hayes, in what would ultimately be his final stint in a professional or semi-professional dugout.

Such was the slump in Hayes' form across Mickey's tenure, we remember being on the bus to a university away match when one of our team-mates found, whilst scrolling social media, a local media poll testing Hayes fans on Mickey's future at the club. 'Should Hayes sack Mickey Lewis?' Despite our best efforts to skew the poll – which can't have had an extensive electorate, leaving it liable to manipulation by a 15-strong bus of ardently pro-Mickey voices – you get the picture of Hayes' fortunes.

But as he grappled with the harsh realities of life without financial support in the Southern Premier League, Mickey was there giving debuts and opportunities to Hayes' youngest players wherever he could. Tristan Lewis talked about one game in particular, against Worthing in the FA Cup. Mickey started with six teenagers. Hayes lost 2-0.

And when Mickey was criticised, as he was after that FA Cup match? When the owner took out his frustrations by complaining that Mickey wore his tracksuit in the bar after the match, rather than the customary shirt and tie? Mickey did what he always did and what few shared his ability to do. He did just what he had done years earlier when Oxford United owner Firoz Kassam had walked into the players' lounge after another Oxford defeat, with a face like thunder, to find Mickey, players and staff commiserating over drinks. He defused the situation, bought everyone a beer and asked: 'What's next?'

Of course, whether consciously or not, he was doing more than just defusing the tension. He was taking the pressure off, even if just for an extra 30 minutes, allowing the young players in his care to enjoy the work they were doing and the people they were doing it with, even in trying times.

In fact, many remember Mickey for this quality above all. And it was a quality for which he clearly commanded a remarkable amount of respect from all those who worked with him. Several suggested they would have 'run through a brick wall' or 'over hot coals' for their touchline 'Mad Dog'.

* * *

So, Mickey had a deep, if perhaps subconscious, understanding of the players who he coached. This was as true for those trying to make their way in the professional game at Oxford United as it was at Hayes and elsewhere. He also knew how to contextualise the work and to take the pressure off when needed. They were qualities for which he rightly commanded great respect.

But it says something further about Mickey that he brought all of himself to assignments that would to others have seemed far less glamorous than a date at Wembley with Oxford United or cup fixtures against Arsène Wenger.

As his employment at Hayes ended and he drifted further from the upper echelons of English football – working with his local Oxfordshire kids' side Stonesfield Strikers and returning to a roster of jobs that included working with some of the worst footballers at the private school Eton College – he kept bringing all of himself to every pitch and every session. His enthusiasm for football and a total absence of ego translated into the training environment Mickey created – an environment that continued to put great stock on hard work, enjoyment and opportunity – regardless of the level at which Mickey was coaching.

Tristan Lewis couldn't help but laugh again at the thought of Mickey, all 5ft 8in of him, with his gruff voice and curly hair, hobbling on to the training field at the country's most exclusive and expensive school or stood in the middle of an unruly circle of the young Stonesfield Strikers. A fair response from anyone observing those sessions might well have been: 'What the fuck is going on?' Or perhaps: 'How the fuck did we get here?'

Tristan Lewis described how Mickey would have every last player on the field in the palm of his hand, within minutes, without fail. He always did.

'Sometimes when you're coaching the little ones, or amateurs, it can feel like a bit of a chore, like "Fucking hell, I've got another session to do." But it didn't matter who Mickey coached. You got the best of him. You never knew if he was having a bad day. You never knew if he was in a bad mood. When he coached, he coached to the best of his ability. That's so rare.'

Paul Charles formed Stonesfield in 2008 and was chairman of the club for many years. His tribute to Mickey is included in full at the back of this book. He decided he was watching a 'maestro' at work soon after watching Mickey coach the juniors for the first time. Someone who 'understands every part'. As far as Charles was and is concerned, 'no one could hold a candle' to the man who ended up giving hours and hours every weekend to the Stonesfield Strikers, from putting the cones out to taking down the nets.

* * *

Perhaps it should be no surprise that Mickey's talent for coaching young players translated so seamlessly beyond professional set-ups like Oxford United. Enjoyment – and his 'don't let it pass you by' philosophy – had always been and remained central to his approach to every training session he ever ran.

This undoubtedly started from within. The fire that had been lit within Mickey as a young West Brom academy player pursuing the ultimate prize of a professional contract seemed to burn brightly throughout his career. Sure, by the time he was coaching Stonesfield and working across the youth game in Oxfordshire, he was no longer a young man. That much was evident from watching him move – perhaps as a consequence of conducting post-match recovery in the pub rather than in the ice bath. But that never stopped him joining in.

There were certainly times with our university side when, as he ran off into the distance after a nutmeg in the rondo, Shearer-esque with his arm in the air in celebration, you weren't sure if he or the joyful cackle was ever going to stop.

Clearly, he grasped and lived something that not many coaches did at the time – that when learning is fun, development happens. He recognised that aggression, tough love and what some might today call 'toxic masculinity' are not necessarily the way to get the best out of people, athletes or otherwise. Of course, there was always a place for a little tough love in Mickey's approach and he dished it out a fair bit, but that was never where his emphasis fell.

Craig Adey worked closely with Mickey at Oxford City and, for a time, took the university second XI. He reiterated this point:

'It can be easy to think that the jovial, jokey Mickey didn't think too hard or deeply about his coaching philosophy. But he knew what his style was. Make sure they're having fun. Make sure they don't have too much time to think too much about it, to get nervous, to worry. The more fun it is, the better they'll play.'

Or, as Ross Weatherstone put it: 'He had a way of coaching, of demonstrating how football should be played and, more importantly, how much fun you should have whilst you're doing it.'

We knew this approach first-hand. As captains of the university side, Mickey would call us at 7am the day after the game and the result was never the main focus of the discussion. It was about what lessons we had learnt and how we would apply them to the next game, and how we could make sure all the players in the squad were getting the most out of their experience.

And it's an approach that has been vindicated in the years since, whether by educational and development psychologists or those working in elite sport. Today, it is entirely normal to hear managers talk about the importance of 'the process' over the result. The England cricket team with their 'Bazball' brand – an all-guns-blazing, spectacular style defined by a maverick and irreverent sense of fun even in the heat of the most competitive battles – is living the philosophy that most of the enjoyment is to be had in the playing of the game and not the discussion of the result, good or bad, at the end of it. The Premier League has coaches now like Tottenham's Ange Postecoglou who talk seriously of focusing on development over results.

* * *

None of that is to reduce Mickey's talent in these situations simply to a passion for football. That is a quality shared in households, on pitchsides and on terraces the length and breadth of the country and, indeed, around the world.

We have already established that Mickey's passion came with a deep technical and tactical understanding of the game and how it was developing and he brought a humility to sharing this with whoever it was he was coaching, no matter the level they were playing.

Former Hayes captain Adam Everitt provided a reminder of Mickey's remarkable ability to impart this deep understanding of the game on to young players, a talent that seems more and more precious in the increasingly jargonistic world of football coaching and analysis – all low blocks, top line runners and baitings of the press. 'I've been in changing rooms where coaches talk, talk, talk. And none of it goes in. Mick was great for young players. He'd just say a couple of things, really simple things.'

All this combined to create an environment for even the most amateur of young players that meant they so profoundly valued the time they spent with Mickey. Why? Because they were being asked to work hard, but they were enjoying themselves and being rewarded with opportunities to grow and develop, too.

Even if they didn't realise it, they were learning to never let it pass them by. And there was one group of unlikely amateurs that took this wisdom particularly to heart.

Chapter 19

'This is their Champions League Final'

MICKEY LEWIS and the University of Oxford. It was, as Mickey himself often remarked with great mischief, an unlikely coupling. The boy from Birmingham who left school to play football, coaching at what is one of the country's most renowned – albeit sometimes reviled – educational institutions.

Now, in matters of football, the university occupies a role that is certainly less contentious or prominent and a little less esteemed, too. Whilst the Boat Race holds on to its prime-time slot on the Thames despite shifting public sentiment, the cricket just about remains at Lord's and the rugby has only just moved away from 82,000-seat Twickenham – played as it was in 2024 at the Saracens ground – the time when the football was played at Wembley is becoming a decades-old memory. The annual match – one of the longest-running regular fixtures in world football – is now usually played at non-league Oxford City's Marsh Lane ground or League One Cambridge United's Abbey Stadium.

For post-season trips to the United States while we were both students, the university donated £1,500 to the tour fund. That figure was put into particularly stark context when our opposition at New York's Columbia University told us that they were building a new athletic complex, funded in part by Google, for tens of millions of dollars. The gulf in funding and quality – we went 5-0 down within the first half – was enormous. Some of the opposition were young men who had played at Inter Milan's academy and might be offered a route to the professional game after college. That wasn't a remote possibility for anyone in Oxford's dark blue, whose professors typically viewed time spent on the football pitch as time frittered away.

But despite the contemporary decline in prestige and the lack of material support for football at the university, Oxford University Association Football Club, known colloquially as OUAFC or 'the Blues', has still played an historic role in the development of English football. OUAFC are one of the oldest clubs in English football and were, in fact, one of the first FA Cup winners. Like the caps given to players who make appearances for the England men's senior team, Oxford players receive jackets for playing against Cambridge in the annual Varsity Match. The team are routinely invited by the world's top universities and teams to compete in their tournaments, to participate in a prestigious pre-season friendly or even to inaugurate stadiums.

So, all that considered, Mickey – the 'bolshie Brummie' whose formal education ended as a teenager when he went professional at West Brom – was probably fair to joke that this particular coaching role was an unlikely turn of events.

* * *

Before Mickey's arrival on the university scene in the summer of 2001, the side had been coached by a combination of Malcolm Crosby – who the squad referred to as 'Crosser' – and Davey Dodds. Crosser had managed Sunderland at Wembley in the 1992 FA Cup Final against Liverpool and, in 2001, he was running the youth team at Swindon while coaching the Blues. Dodds was the academy manager at Reading. So, Crosser and Dodds were two serious coaches.

But what happened next still defied logic. Dodds moved to Watford in 2001. So, the university first team needed a new coach. But it wasn't to be Mickey's time just yet. Dodds had a different suggestion: Chelsea, Juventus and Italy legend Gianluca Vialli.

The Vialli era – which lasted about 33 coaching hours, or as long as was necessary for him to complete the first stage of his FA level one badge – is a brief departure from the story of Mickey's coaching of young players, but it requires recounting in full.

Vialli is widely recognised as one of the game's greats and also one of its genuine nice guys. In his playing career, he won almost everything there was to win in European football: the European Cup, Serie A, the FA Cup, the League Cup, the Coppa Italia and several top scorer awards to top it off. This ought to have been enough for Watford, a Championship club who had just finished bottom of the Premier League. But the FA was clear: a badge is a badge. And so, Vialli had to undertake his FA level one coaching course before taking up the reins at Vicarage Road.

Luckily for the students in the squad at the time, Vialli found the Blues. It was another classic example of the irony and sometimes absurdity of the university football set-up, which had previously boasted Sir Bobby Robson as a coach, albeit also briefly; starry-eyed 20-somethings with an overdue essay finding themselves on the pitch with a bona fide legend.

Brendan McGurk from the squad of the time remembers the night when Steve Rishworth, the Blues captain in 2001, spoke to Vialli on the phone for the first time. The whole squad had gathered for a meal at a flat in the quaint Oxford neighbourhood of Jericho. They were in the middle of watching *Gladiator* when the call from Vialli came in. There were hushed giggles and whispers as Rishworth quietened down the lads and put the phone to his ear, ready to put on his serious voice.

It seemed like Rishworth was finishing up after a few minutes of conversation. An exciting moment for all those patiently waiting, straining to hear the voice on the other end of the line. But before he hung up the phone, he added, confidently: 'Cheers, Luca.'

'Howls of laughter broke the collective silence when Steve ended the call with that,' McGurk said. 'It was like they had been best mates for years. A glorious moment.'

Vialli agreed to run a few sessions at the Iffley Road astroturf, though he certainly wasn't going to drive himself there nor arrive in a car full of footballs and scrunched-up coaching notes like Mickey would go on to do some years later. No, Vialli turned up in what one player described as a 'bullet-proof black Bentley' and then 'chain-smoked at the side of the pitch'. The sessions were very attack-focused – like Mickey's – and occasionally Vialli took part himself. The players could have been forgiven for thinking this was all some sort of curious fever dream.

The situation became clearer when the lads found out that Dodds was effectively in the middle of a glorified job interview for a coaching role at Watford, under Vialli's new leadership. That was perhaps unsurprising. The university players at the time remembered Dodds as an excellent coach. A 'technician who, one sensed, brought the same drills to the university side as he ran as a professional coach'.

Once Vialli completed his course – ending his short association with the university side as he did so – he didn't take long before offering Dodds a job at Watford. So, going into the 2001/02 season, the Blues needed a new coach.

* * *

The Oxford players had enjoyed their time with 'Luca'. And his presence had only added to the sense amongst the squad of the time of the calibre of coach the club should be attracting, especially given this was just over a decade after the last Varsity Match was played at Wembley and for much of the 1990s that game had been played at Craven Cottage, a Premier League stadium.

The players of that period were also not complete no-hopers. The side at the time included Old Etonian James Redmayne, brother of Oscar-winner Eddie, who was one of the rare holders of both a football and cricket 'Blue', the award received for performing in the university's first team in a given sport. Former schoolboy pro Chris Woodcock was also there. He had apparently once been chosen ahead of Steven Gerrard for a Lilleshall training camp and was destined for a bright future at Newcastle United before injury struck. So, for the next manager of one of English football's oldest clubs, a big name was expected.

Enter, Mickey Lewis. With Oxford United and Oxford City associations already under his belt, it was time for him to complete a curious, but undoubtedly unprecedented, Oxford triple.

Well, sort of. It nearly wasn't to be. Physics student Kevin Costello was trying to secure Mickey's services. He had met Mickey once and they had exchanged details, so he and the squad were hopeful of recruiting 'Mr Oxford Football'.

Mickey had given Costello a three-day window in which to call and discuss the role. Costello called. Mickey didn't answer. That happened again. And again. By the 12th call, real concern was growing that Mickey had changed his mind and had taken another job. He was, after all, known for his extensive portfolio of coaching jobs across the Oxfordshire area and the Blues were asking for a fair amount of his time to take coaching three or four times a week, as well as their matches on Wednesday afternoons.

When Mickey called Costello back at the end of day three to tell him that he was so sorry, he'd been away on holiday with his wife, and yes, of course he'd love to take the job, it was a huge relief.

* * *

And so, Mickey's long love affair with the University of Oxford team began.

The first impressions were impressive. 'You could immediately tell he had been a highly accomplished player. His touch on the ball during sessions was exquisite, as were the signature 40-yard, half-volleyed pings with the outside of his right boot,' said one of that 2001/02 squad. We can confirm. By the time we were in his team, some decade-and-a-half later, Mickey could still ping a ball on the half-volley with the outside of his right boot. And he never let us forget it.

And whilst results didn't come immediately in Mickey's first season, his approach to the job quickly became celebrated. And how exactly he went about the work is a familiar story.

The university sessions were often uncomfortably early or late to fit around Mickey's full-time commitments and the Wednesday afternoon matches were often in far-flung parts of the country, but he never gave the impression the work was a chore. And he showed immediately that he cared for the role and the young players in his charge, as he always did.

Even in those early seasons, when Mickey was working several courier jobs across Oxford to keep money coming in after hanging up his boots, he bounded into the training sessions with the kind of enthusiasm that had become his hallmark as a player. On days Mickey couldn't attend training due to another commitment, he would often send a handwritten note for the captain to read out before the session or match began.

Having played for Mickey in the early days of his time with the university, Brendan McGurk remembered that Mickey would always start a Friday session after a game he'd had to miss by asking the team how they'd played and genuinely working to understand what had gone well or badly. 'Heard you bagged one – in the air?' McGurk told us that 'you had a very real sense that this was a guy who could get on with anyone and could adapt to any coaching set-up'. And just as he did on every training pitch where he worked, he showed that intuitive appreciation of the importance of combining hard work and fun, and a focus on tactical and technical development, trusting as he did that results would follow. All whilst demonstrating that remarkable adeptness for communication.

McGurk described the sessions as 'akin to what a kids' coach would do: last pair into a group of three did press-ups; last to pair with someone, press-ups; line-up, right means left and left means right, get it wrong, press-ups'. But there was a 'method in his madness'. It was fun and 'every drill, most of which were played out in a deliberately condensed space, was geared not just to be competitive, but to ensure that we were switched on 100 per cent of the time, even when fatigued'.

Captain some years later in the 2015/16 season, Laurence Wroe recalled a particular piece of wisdom that Mickey imparted during one of his typically intense sessions. He's long graduated, even if, by his own admission, he is one of a few to fall for a plea Mickey made to many players in the Blues as they faced their graduation date: 'Oh, come on mate, just do another degree.' He has since gone on to work as a nuclear physicist at CERN, the world's largest particle accelerator, in Switzerland. But even now, Wroe remembers Mickey barking: 'Space never scored a goal. You never see Arsenal one Spurs nil, goal scored by space, do you?'

And if Mickey wasn't shouting about space's inability to score a goal, he was often barking about something he'd seen in the highlights from a recent Premier League match. Perhaps something like Agüero or Ibrahimović having earned the right to score by running the channel – the spaces behind opposition full-backs where an attacker might run, mainly to create space and scoring opportunities for their striking partner – something he was particularly fond of encouraging his attackers to do, often against their wishes.

'No one's too good to run the channel,' he would tell those attackers. In other words, no one is above working hard for the benefit of the team. Equal parts mischievous and straightforwardly profound.

It is no surprise, then, that virtually every player from that early period – and, indeed, from all the squads since – talk about training with Mickey as the happiest times of their university lives. And it wasn't just the players who thrived in his presence. Craig Adey, who took on the university second team in 2018 at Mickey's request, remembers time spent with Mickey on the grass with the university side as fondly as any of the players.

For Adey, who made the fair point that the late Friday training slot could easily have been a graveyard shift and the Sunday morning session a hassle, Mickey's enthusiasm was infectious: 'I miss those mornings. As much as I love coaching the university guys, it was him I woke up for on a Sunday morning. I wouldn't have done it for any other man.'

* * *

Thanks in no small part to this approach to training, an improvement in on-pitch fortunes soon followed.

As winter turned to spring in the 2001/02 season – Mickey's first in charge – his squad went on a run of only one defeat in 13 games. And as that first season ended with an initial threat of relegation avoided, there was one final order of business to attend to.

Mickey's first ever Varsity Match – the pinnacle of many university careers – took place in late March 2002 at Queens Park Rangers' Loftus Road in west London. Not Wembley, but not bad. And the players made a trip to London the night before, getting a taste of the professional game as they stayed and prepared in the Kensington Hilton.

But they were not, of course, professionals. They were students. Students who might be comfortable in an exam hall but who had likely never walked out in front of a crowd of thousands, as they would do in the morning. So, Mickey came down from his hotel room to dinner and found a squad racked with a nervousness somewhat alien to someone as steeped in the professional game as he was.

He called Suzanne, who knew exactly what to say. 'This is their Champions League Final,' she told him.

That was all Mickey needed to hear. That night, he distracted the squad with every card game in his arsenal and sent them off to bed with the game much further from their minds than it had been earlier in the evening. And, in absorbing the importance of the occasion to his players, he did so in a way that other past masters of the professional game might have felt beneath them. After that night in the hotel playing cards with the squad, 'it was as big for him as it was for the lads', Suzanne recalls.

As for the match itself? Well, it followed the globally renowned Boat Race, in which the Oxford crew had won one of the tightest and most exciting races in the occasion's 120-year history. *The Times* reported that 'there was no such high-octane drama' in the football Varsity.

The final result was 0-0 after a turgid 90 minutes and, in the era with no penalty shoot-out and no trophy handed out in the event of a tie, both teams went home more than a little disappointed.

As Brendan McGurk noted with a smile:

'As if the 1,500 or so supporters hadn't suffered enough during the 90 minutes of stalemate, at full time news came over the Tannoy that the Queen Mother had died and the post-match medals were mournfully presented to both teams by Jimmy Hill, one of Mickey's predecessors as coach of the Blues.'

This annual occasion became, from that point on, an important part of Mickey's story. In fact, Mickey went on to be – as far as records show – one of the most successful coaches in the history of the fixture. The next three years following the 0-0 draw saw three Oxford victories to nil, giving Oxford the upper hand in the overall head-to-head record in a fixture that stretches back to 1873. It is a head-to-head lead that Oxford has maintained ever since.

* * *

As Mickey fell into the rhythm of the university footballing calendar, he absorbed himself in the quirks and idiosyncrasies that came with it.

As one of the club's class of 2003 told us: 'He took it all in his stride, even when an American TV news crew followed the team on a Sunday morning run, eager to get a shot of Ian Klaus, the then boyfriend of Oxford student Chelsea Clinton [daughter of Bill and Hillary].'

The squad would often go for Sunday lunch at Vincent's, the members' club open to university athletes, and Mickey would join them. When any more formal functions came around, Mickey donned his jacket and sunk several – pints with the team.

He didn't seem to mind at all that the squad was typically made up of a curious assortment of personalities. Certainly a far cry from a typical professional football squad. As Chris Wilder remembers: 'He loved coaching the university, working with different types of people, different types of players.'

Wilder joined Mickey and the university squad in the pub after a training session. Wilder found himself sitting next to one of the postgraduates in the team, a young man who he described as one of the country's foremost experts on British earthquakes:

> 'I'm looking at him and thinking, "Fucking hell, how many times a year do you come into action?" Any time Britain has an earthquake, he gets rolled out, the why and where and what. For fuck's sake, that's got to be the easiest job in the world.'

You can probably see where this is going. Two months after that pub trip, England *did* experience an earthquake. A mild one. But an earthquake, nonetheless. There was Wilder at home, watching the news with his toast and marmalade, seeing his drinking companion providing the country with the lowdown on what had happened.

Mickey would keep in regular touch with many of the players who passed through the squad, long after they'd graduated and moved away from Oxford.

Dom Affron was the university's second XI captain a few years into Mickey's time with the club. He regularly trained with the first team and he and Mickey were training ground sparring partners. Affron, a Baggies fan, provided a foil to Mickey and his enthusiasm for Birmingham City, the club he used to go to as a kid with his dad.

A year or two after Affron had graduated, West Brom drew Oxford United in the League Cup. The tie was to be played at The Hawthorns and Affron would be attending. Thinking of Mickey in the away dugout, Affron texted his old coach to wish him luck for the 'Mickey Lewis derby'. Mickey, who surely had matchday preparations to attend to in his role with United, fired back instantly: 'Thanks mate. I'll let you know if we're short on players.'

* * *

It wasn't just the company that was quirky. So, too, was the politics of the university 'Blue'. A Blue is, according to the university, 'the highest honour granted to individual sportspeople at the University of Oxford and is a highly sought-after achievement for Oxford student athletes'. Each sport at Oxford has different criteria for the winning of a Blue. But for the football team, competing in a Varsity Match will get you over the line. Alongside the honour and pride, students receive a navy blue blazer with the football club's crest woven into the breast pocket, which becomes the uniform of choice at any current player or alumni function in the years that follow.

But, of course, this condition – the requirement to actually *compete* in the Varsity Match – means only 14 or 15 of a 16- or 18-person squad can go home happy.

That simply wouldn't do for Mickey. While many coaches may have accepted the natural order of things, Mickey tried to make sure that as many players as possible got the recognition that he felt they deserved. Mark Addley told us of one such occasion. In one of the first Varsity Matches of Mickey's time in charge of the club, at the Abbey Stadium in 2004, a young man called Pat Walker had been selected as a substitute goalkeeper. With a few minutes remaining and with Oxford hanging on for a 1-0 win, Mickey brought him on to play on the left side of defence.

Oxford did hang on and any initially raised eyebrows turned into hearty, beer-fuelled laughter in the Abbey clubhouse. Mickey confessed to the lads that he had made a list of those players for whom this would be their final Varsity Match and who had yet to win a Blue. It was a practice he maintained throughout the course of his time in the role.

Mickey always balanced this slight sentimentality with his ever-present competitiveness. In that first Varsity Match, one of the team's key men was in a lot of pain and seemed unable to play. Mickey wasn't having it. He spoke to the physio he had brought along for the game – the Blues did not usually have a physio, unless you count a twice-a-season masseuse – and the physio then offered the player something presented as an extreme strength analgesic.

The player popped the pill, warmed up, came back in and said that, despite being a tad dizzy, he was pain-free and would be fine to play. In the bar after the game, with a 1-0 victory secured and goalkeeper Pat Walker celebrating his involvement, Mickey revealed to the player that he told the physio to give him paracetamol.

Years later, during the 2018 Varsity Match – in which both of us played and one of us (the one that scored the second goal) was subbed off for not tracking back in the 70th minute – one observer remembers Mickey 'still jumping out of his seat urging more effort, even with a three-nil lead'. And it wasn't just his own players who would benefit from Mickey's competitive instincts. One young player recalls Mickey, wrapped up in the moment on the touchline, encouraging him to target a Cambridge defender's 'pony left foot'. Another remembers Mickey screaming 'let him have it, let him have it', when a weak opposition defender dithered on the ball, assuring his team that 'he'll give it back to you'. Which, of course, he did. 'You see, there you go.' And others still remember him giving 90-minute-long earfuls to the likes of Martin Atkinson, Paul Tierney and Craig Pawson, the Premier League referees who have at various points taken charge of the Varsity Match.

* * *

The Varsity Match wasn't the only showpiece event in the club's annual calendar. Each summer, except for when funds were exceptionally low, when the captain was exceptionally disorganised or when the world was shut down by a pandemic, the squad usually went on tour.

And so it was at the end of the 2007/08 season, when one of the Czech Republic's most successful sides, Slavia Prague, invited the university to be their opposition in a friendly to open their brand new stadium, the Stadion Eden. The university had been the first English team to play Slavia, back in 1899, so it seemed a natural fit for the auspicious occasion.

Fresh off the back of a 5-3 defeat in that year's Varsity Match at Craven Cottage and not quite believing their luck, a side of current players and recently graduated alumni assembled – to make up a squad that was surely oversubscribed – and met for a single training session before the flight.

Mickey wasn't actually in charge in the 2007/08 season. That year's captain was presented with his Vialli opportunity, as Arsenal 'Invincible' and Oxford landlord Martin Keown made himself available for the job, similarly in search of his own coaching badges. There was not room for two fairly well-remunerated, former professional footballers on the coaching staff, and so Mickey focused his attention elsewhere.

It was a surreal year. Long after the shine had faded from the fixture, Keown's involvement brought renewed media interest. *The Telegraph* wrote up an interview with Keown on the eve of the fixture, in which Keown lamented the style of play, remembered an away match for which the squad had forgotten the kit and also set out the lengths he had gone to in order to professionalise the squad.

'Training every day, eating properly,' training sessions exactly as Wenger had run them, pre-match naps and a no-alcohol charter were all on the list. 'To beat Cambridge you don't just turn up tomorrow, you turn up now,' Keown barked at his players during the training session the *Telegraph* journalist observed.

But such a big name has a big schedule and, having fallen out with the captain and seen his side thrashed by Cambridge on their big day at Craven Cottage, he couldn't make it down to the pre-Prague session in Oxford. In stepped Mickey, who came in and reunited with many of the players who were already so fond of him.

It seems unlikely that Keown left a handwritten note for the session as Mickey usually would have done when he couldn't be there in person. In fact, Leon Farr remembers – with an impressively diplomatic tone – that 'it could be said that some aspects of [Keown's] sessions didn't translate well to amateur players who perhaps weren't blessed with the first touch of Dennis Bergkamp or the passing ability of Patrick Vieira'.

Farr ended up being one of the lucky few to make the touring squad and remembers the time well:

'Mickey generously agreed to step in at the last minute. When I heard that Martin couldn't make it, I was nervous. I'd never met Mickey and we had very little time to prepare for a match in front of 15,000 spectators. Within minutes of the session starting, though, I knew we were in safe hands. Mickey did some defensive shape work with us – knowing, of course, that we would have absolutely none of the ball in the match – and his knowledge was immediately obvious.

'This was not someone who needed time to win over cocky students and build their trust – there was an instant breezy authority. "Don't worry about the Hollywood pass!" he barked, encouraging the winger and full-back to tuck in and shift across with the ball. "If he makes that switch of play, I'll hold my hands up, but he's not Glenn Hoddle!"'

Neither Farr nor any of his team-mates were under any illusions about the scale of the task that awaited them. As Farr continued:

'Goalkeeper Dave Robinson reminded Mickey that, although Slavia wouldn't be fielding Glenn Hoddle, they could well be fielding several full internationals, which got a smile out of Mickey. He knew he was sending lambs to the slaughter, but I still went into that game feeling more confident. Later, I laughed with Mickey about Vladimír Šmicer and Patrick Berger relentlessly pinging perfect "Hollywood" passes over our heads as Slavia dispatched us 5-0 (and it could have been any score they wanted). Turns out even Mickey couldn't bridge the gap between student amateurs and top-level pros in a single training session!'

* * *

As his tenure with the university progressed into its second decade, Mickey would come to talk about the work as some of the most enjoyable of his career. Suzanne suggested that he enjoyed working with the Blues so much because of the mutual respect he felt with the players: 'They were at the top of their game academically, so they respected somebody who was at the top of theirs. They listened, they wanted to get better.'

And whilst it might well have been an unlikely situation, Mickey thrived in it, cementing his status as one of, if not *the*, most successful manager in the club's storied history. The late Oxford professor Stuart Ferguson, who was involved with the club for much of the last half-decade, drew a comparison to the period that ran from the 1950s through to the late 1970s, with the Varsity Match often played at Wembley Stadium, where the Oxford side barely won at all. Mickey's was, as Ferguson called it, 'a job very well done indeed'. And he was so successful with the university for so long for exactly the reasons he was so successful with young players across Oxfordshire and across football.

Whilst some argue that being too likeable as a manager is a fatal flaw, at the university it was Mickey's likeability, his strong relationships with those he coached and his warmth that made him so effective. Brendan McGurk put it neatly:

'His reputation as a player and coach, and how he treated each and every one of us, garnered enormous respect and, indeed, affection. He did not seek out friendship, but every one of us believed that he was a friend. He was always approachable and would always listen. He knew enough about each of us to always be able to ask about things beyond football. He walked the difficult line between being the coach rather than one of the lads, yet always remaining hugely popular.'

Perhaps it was easier to walk that line in the unique environment of university football, where contracts aren't on the line, players aren't supporting families, tens of thousands of people aren't pinning their weekly mood on your Saturday result and there are (for the most part) no disparaging newspaper columns.

But, regardless, the fact remains that those university players that we've spoken to and have played with all comment on the fact that playing for the Blues, walking out at Loftus Road or

Craven Cottage – and doing it all under Mickey's leadership – was the highlight of their footballing career. For many, it was a formative experience in their life.

And, crucially, Mickey knew this. That meant he was able to show all those playing for him that it meant a hell of a lot to him, too. As Phil Heath said: 'He just loved being with the lads so much. It's not about money, it's about prestige. He loved that aspect.'

It was simply football. For football's sake.

Chapter 20

'Up for anything, into anything, there for anyone'

SO, WHETHER at Oxford United, in non-league football, at the university or with the young ones at clubs like Stonesfield, the positive influence that Mickey had on young men and boys he coached and mentored was profound.

And there was one final place where that was true: the Velocity programme that Mickey ran out of Oxford City.

These were late teenagers, 18 and 19, based at City's Marsh Lane complex – where the university side also trained and often played – playing football alongside a sports- and business-based college education. Many of them were from vulnerable backgrounds. They often lacked support at home and many had already once turned their back on college, just as the education system had turned its back on all too many of them. Football, really, was a singular release.

It was Mickey who stepped up for the boys at Velocity, as he so often did. The same days he spent working with the university squad, many of whom had come from the most prestigious schools in the country and who'd been afforded a series of significant advantages, he also spent with some of the country's least fortunate.

Those who worked with him as part of the programme describe, without exception, an environment in which he treated all the boys in the programme as the young men they were, with respect and as equals.

That didn't mean he wasn't as demanding and tough as usual. He wanted the best for everyone he coached and, as he'd shown consistently throughout his coaching career, he was realistic enough about the world beyond Velocity to know that no one would benefit from an easy ride. But he married those demands on his players with a respect and kindness that too many of them hadn't before received.

Mary Page worked at Oxford United for the best part of four decades and she remembers this aspect of Mickey's style well. 'He was strict when he needed to be. He wouldn't have any nonsense. But he was fair, he would listen. If a player had got problems, if anybody had a problem, they could always turn to Mickey.'

In the simplest terms, the boys in the Velocity programme knew Mickey had their back. That was true on the pitch and on the training ground. It was true if they had something on their mind from home. If they had a problem with their college work, he'd be sure to give that a crack as well.

And it wasn't just the young players he looked out for. Those who worked with him noted his immense care and respect for the young coaches around him, too. Paul Wanless, who was an Oxford United trainee in the early 1990s, explained why Mickey had such a positive reputation amongst the coaches he worked with:

'Mickey galvanised people in the right way, the quiet way. You just followed him. And you know why? Because there was absolutely zero ego and arrogance. We would get together later in life and he would always tell me about the positive things the coaches at Oxford City were doing. Mickey never ever once would say anything bad about the lads coaching the boys.'

* * *

So, what have we learned here?

It is accepted now that young men, especially young male footballers, need firm but caring role models to show them the way, to recognise that they need love as much as they need tactical or technical advice and to see when they need a tough word when they are pushing their luck. Mickey was exactly that for thousands of young players, all of whom got the same treatment – the same fair chance, the same arm around the shoulder, the same kick up the backside. He was, as Oxford United groundsman Mick Moore put it, there for everyone and anyone, all the time.

It explains why so many of the young men and boys that he coached described him as a father figure. He took these players by the hand and led them into an adulthood in which they would be better footballers, but also in which they were better prepared for everything else. For all that their personal and professional lives might throw at them.

And there was that one line that Mickey often reserved for young players and deployed to particular effect. He said it to both of us several times per week and even more often when the big occasions rolled around: 'Don't let the game pass you by.'

On the surface, he was referring to the 90 minutes in front of us. He was talking about the first tackle of the match, where we would let the other team know we were there, early doors. He was nudging us to work a little harder, run a little further, do a little more for your team-mates. And those words surely fuelled some 90th-minute goals and goal-saving tackles.

But, with time, we've come to learn what Mickey really meant, as have so many of those interviewed for this book. He was telling us – all of us – to look around and appreciate how lucky we were to be playing the game we all loved amongst our closest friends. He was reminding us that nothing in life is ever guaranteed. And he was instilling in us the idea that opportunities are there for us and how we use them is in our hands.

SECTION THREE:

ENJOY THE OCCASION

Chapter 21

The West Bromwich Albion Department of Justice

'Mickey was a great mover, a great dancer.'

Mary Page, long-time member of the
Oxford United staff

*'I'd say more of an enthusiastic
mover than a dancer.'*

Phil Gilchrist, team-mate at Oxford United

MICKEY LEWIS was a man who took seriously his obligation not just to play and coach the game, but also to enjoy the occasion. More or less any occasion. Doing so was a natural continuation of his commitment to never let it – football or life – pass him or those around him by.

Of course, Mickey played and then moved into coaching before Arsène Wenger had arrived in English football, bringing with him a worldview and management style built on quality nutrition and robust sports science, rather than alcohol, bad diets and various other off-pitch distractions. And so, for much of Mickey's career, he was working at a time in which there was ample opportunity to celebrate the highs, commiserate the lows and mark all the various other waypoints in between. By the time Wenger had arrived and most aspects of the game began to rapidly modernise, one might argue that the die was long cast: Mickey liked to have a good time.

So, what follows in this section is an entirely true account of Mickey's raucous and hilarious life lived away from the pitch.* And, in homage to the manner in which that life was lived, it is an account that leans heavily on anecdote, good humour and the help of plenty of fine raconteurs.

Entirely true, that is, insofar as it was possible for those around Mickey to have even the vaguest recollection of the stories they were recounting.

* * *

To tell the story of Mickey off the pitch, we have to go back again to the start of his career, at the West Brom academy. As Mickey was making the jump from Birmingham's amateur leagues and working his way through the Albion youth set-up, he found a firm friend in Peter Frain. The two of them were inseparable as they travelled across town for training and matches. They looked after each other on the pitch. And they took their camaraderie beyond the Midlands to Europe, with their England youth team in their late teenage years.

But what about after their training sessions and matches? What happened once they'd sweated it out and were getting thirsty? Well, Mickey and Frain – both Acocks Green boys – fast became drinking partners, too.

'We were just being introduced to girls,' recalls Frain. 'We'd go on double dates to the local pub next to Mick's place, have a couple of glasses of beer just for us, a couple of glasses of wine with the girls and then we would have to get up for training the next day.'

It's not totally clear whether they were using fake IDs or if it was just that the local pub turned a blind eye to academy boys. But what's certain is that, from a young age, they were both learning the importance of savouring life off the pitch as much as on it.

As they got older and closer to the first team, which would have had a drinking culture of its own, befitting of the late 1970s and early 1980s in English football, the two of them showed no sign of slowing down.

At 16 and 17, in the summer of 1982, the two of them were part of the West Brom youth team that was on tour in Germany. They were the bedrock of both the starting XI and the dressing-room atmosphere, and Frain hasn't forgotten the way they ruled the roost: 'We'd hold kangaroo courts. Mick would be the prosecutor, I'd be the judge. If you came up against us, it didn't matter what you'd done.'

And so it was for two of the young lads in the side, on their first European tour, who got lucky and met a couple of young ladies out and about after one of the tour matches. The two of them took their new friends for a drink in a German beer hall, went for a romantic stroll at sunset and even got a kiss before saying goodnight. Living the dream. Or they were, until Mickey and Peter caught wind of their antics back at the hotel.

Court was immediately in session. Mickey, the prosecutor, asked the first question:

> 'Right lads, what's this all about? Buying chocolate on tour for ladies? Riverside walks after the sun has gone down? Kisses? Really? This is unacceptable behaviour for young club ambassadors, lads!'

Giggles were surely rippling through the squad as Mickey worked at maintaining a straight face.

Frain, the judge, interrupted: 'I've heard enough. I've seen enough. These lads are on the road to ruin if they don't mend their ways soon. I've no choice but to hand them a suspended sentence, with an immediate obligation to go and buy all the food for the team for the rest of the trip.'

At this point there were surely howls of laughter from the rest of the team and perhaps good-humoured groans from the young lads. There were undoubtedly wicked smiles from the West Bromwich Albion youth team's Department of Justice.

And what were their names, these two unwitting whippersnappers? We'll preserve their anonymity. But Mickey and Frain called them Harris and Sketchly. Why? Because, in 1982, these were two of the UK's largest cleaning companies. Why, you ask again? Because, as Judge Frain made clear in his closing statement, the lads had been taken to the cleaners! Obviously.

Poor things. All they'd done was found some nice girls on holiday, bought them some chocolate and a drink or two, and given them a polite kiss before bedtime. Not so innocent for Mickey and Frain, the two big brothers making sure the younger upstarts didn't get too big for their boots.

So, it seems fair to conclude that, from early on, Mickey was something of a troublemaker? Phil Heath, Oxford United team-mate and Mickey's best man, provided a careful answer to that particular suggestion: 'Well, how do I put this? He was a troublemaker, but he never got into trouble.'

Chapter 22

'Right, go home lads,
you're in turmoil'

THOSE WHO knew Mickey later in his career might think of him as a man unbothered about his image.

When he opened his car door before a training session, out spilled cones, bibs and other debris collected across the years he'd been driving the car. By his 40s, he had a distinctive hobble, courtesy of a body battered and bruised across two decades as a combative defensive midfielder.

And he always wore more or less the same coaching attire – his black boots, blue shorts or baggy blue tracksuit bottoms, faded jumper, raincoat – whilst regularly reminding people, with a fair amount of pride, that he only had two haircuts a year.

It was not always so.

As Mickey was building his professional career back in the late 1970s and 1980s, footballers weren't necessarily fashion icons. David Beckham hadn't yet appeared in Emporio Armani campaigns. Players weren't gracing the cover of *GQ* or fashion week red carpets as they do today. But this was the era of the Mods and Rockers. Of The Jam and Eric Clapton. Of the Bryan Robson perm. Diego Maradona landed at Heathrow in 1986 wearing a designer jumper and a long gold chain. He skied in the Argentinian resort Las Lenas in a blue Benetton jumper and jeans paired with a glitzy silver chain. So, in their own ways, players of the time took their appearances seriously and Mickey was no different.

Local Oxford journalist Jerome Sale remembers him as a player who would appear for his post-match interview in his shirt and tie:

> 'He was a sharp dresser, dapper, in the fashion of the time, with his big white paisley ties, absolutely stinking of aftershave. You'd do an interview at five, ten past, and by six o'clock, you'd still be able to smell where he'd been.'

And so it was, with the crisp shirt, suave tie and pungent cologne all over his face, neck and wrists, that the revelry could begin.

* * *

Team-mates and friends of Mickey's lined up to share their memories of the time they spent with him in pubs and clubs or on away trips. That was especially true for those who knew Mickey from his time as a player at Oxford, where he'd really grown from youth player to man.

Team-mate and best man Phil Heath remembers his time in the Oxford squad with Mickey as if they were schoolboys staying away from home on a school trip.

'He loved all the lads being together. And one of the best things about him, he always had this capacity to invent a game, from anything. Even when he'd just signed, we were away at Swansea and he just took over the activities completely. Everyone completely adored him for that.'

Mickey was the ringmaster, just as he had been as a West Brom youngster. If there was time to fill, he'd find a way to fill it. With card games or with umbrella golf clubs for hotel corridor tournaments. He'd sometimes even take his own cricket bat on away days or on tour, particularly if he knew there was a beach nearby. If there was a kitty to be run or fines to be distributed, he'd be there running the book. If there was a kangaroo court to organise, just as the poor West Brom youngsters found out on tour in Germany, he'd be judge, jury and executioner.

Team-mate Jim Magilton remembers that the fun even extended on to long afternoons and evenings on the team coach. As Magilton described for a raucous episode of Oxford United's club podcast, which he recorded with his old midfield partner, Mickey needed no encouragement to get up on the tables of the coach, to start flexing a John Travolta impression that many – if not all! – remember as second to none.

Of course, as soon as the opportunity presented itself, on the away days or just off the coach back in Oxford, Mickey would lead the charge to the pub, too.

'Oh yeah, we had some proper nights,' Phil Heath told us. 'I was a bit of a lightweight. I was definitely not his wingman. He was just ferocious. He could go for hours. He did the Pinky and the Perky [Oxford's lethal drink, a pint-sized glass of grapefruit juice, orange juice and five shots of either vodka or gin] and put them away in minutes.'

On one occasion some years later, during which Mickey was several Pinkies down, he apparently spent 45 minutes trying to find his way out of the club he'd been dragged to by the university students. Though Mickey never told us about this one.

* * *

Heath and Anton Rogan – who'd go on to have a stellar Celtic and Northern Ireland career – were two of Mickey's most committed drinking partners.

Rogan fondly remembers long afternoons, even longer nights and the hungover mornings that followed in his little flat in Middle Way, which Mickey often retired to after their biggest sessions.

If there was any doubt about exactly how they were living at the time, Rogan remembers Mickey complaining of his hunger after one evening of revelry, opening the fridge and seeing nothing more than a spare rib and a chocolate Santa. You can almost hear Rogan asking, in his thick Northern Irish accent and after a well-timed beat for comic effect: 'Lewy, what do you want, son?'

'Rog, I'll have the chocolate Santa, please, you have the rib,' replied Mickey, equally deadpan. And Heath chuckled to himself as he recounted the occasion of breaking his leg during a reserve-team match away at Ipswich Town. Not the most amusing of set-ups for a story, you might be thinking. That is, of course, until Mickey got involved.

Mickey's first task was to pick up Heath from the John Radcliffe Hospital in Oxford after he'd been seen and plastered. Heath had decided Mickey was a safer bet than his mum and dad, who lived a couple of hours away in Stoke-on-Trent, given he was in the hospital until the early hours of the following morning.

Mickey was more than happy to help. He even took it upon himself to ensure Heath didn't miss out on any valuable social time as a result of his injury, assuming the role of taxi driver to and from whichever pub it was the squad was aiming for after training or a match.

By the summer – the match at Ipswich had fallen in one of the final weeks of the season – Mickey and Heath were off to Marbella. The pair headed immediately to the beach, Mickey still playing a sort of taxi, carrying Heath to the sun loungers. He decided the jetty 30 yards out to sea looked like a perfect resting spot.

'Come on Heathy, I'll carry you,' Mickey said, confidently.

And he did, for a moment. Until he dropped Heath in the water.

Whether it was deliberate or not remains open to debate. Heath takes a neutral stance. Either way, Mickey found the whole saga hilarious and continued to do so for the rest of the trip, even as Heath lay prone on his hotel room bed, waiting for Mickey to take the hairdryer to the sodden, barely functioning plaster cast.

* * *

Of course, Heath, Rogan and Mickey rarely drank alone. This was the late 1980s and early 1990s. Drinking was basically written into the playing contracts.

And one particularly famous – or infamous – story from this time is that of the Oxford United 'cowboys and Indians' Christmas party.

The squad was allowed to finish training early, at lunchtime. Each of them swiftly ran off to ready themselves for the afternoon and evening's festivities, with particular attention paid to preparing their fancy dress. Half the team were dressed as cowboys, the other half were Indians. Or, as we would, of course, now prefer, Native Americans.

The meeting point was the White Horse, one of central Oxford's most famous pubs and allegedly an old favourite of authors C.S. Lewis and J.R.R. Tolkien. A route from there was plotted through many of the city's most famous drinking holes. By mid-afternoon, the squad had arrived at the Coach & Horses, still fully committed to their outfits and certainly in full voice.

Rogan remembers that just as he was the ringleader of the cowboys, Mickey – or Lewy, as Rogan still calls him – was the ringleader of the Native Americans.

'Next thing I know, Lewy separates everybody. And he just starts fucking throwing things. He's got all the cowboys trapped in this circle and he's got his lads running around the outside, throwing sausage rolls, throwing sandwiches. He's got this big tomahawk, which he's shaking up in the air.'

One wonders what the Coach & Horses regulars made of the spectacle. Rogan insists they 'just left us to it'. A swift exit stage left seems a likelier story.

This was all still mid-afternoon. The rest of the day must have flashed past in a drunken haze, since none of the players seem to remember where they went next or what they did.

And as for the morning after?

Defender Phil Gilchrist insisted that the squad were usually very much able to handle their drink. The sweat and the smell of alcohol were usually the only things that indicated it hadn't been a quiet night in front of the television. And Mickey had a particular reputation as a brilliant escape artist, capable of training at full tilt whether hungover or not.

Heath remembers one session in which he was trying to win back his place in the team, so hadn't joined the chaos of the evening before, and found himself feeling quite smug as the rest of the squad, including Mickey, stumbled into training very clearly hungover. His smugness quickly turned to disbelief as Mickey and the other revellers tore through the session and Heath found himself on the receiving end of a hammering from manager Brian Horton in the post-session sauna for missing a chance near the end of the small-sided match. Mickey did apparently leap to Heath's defence, pointing out that he himself had been steaming for the entirety of the session, but the point stands.

Despite this clear talent for putting the night before behind them, Mickey and the squad had no such luck during the morning session after the cowboys Christmas party. The training was a short-lived affair and Rogan vividly remembers the manager's assessment: 'Right, go home lads, you're in turmoil.'

The manager in question, Brian Horton, seems to have entirely expunged the memory. He did, however, make a comment that captures perfectly what enjoying the occasion was all about: 'I don't really remember the story, to be honest with you. But I'll tell you something …'

You can probably guess what's next.

'Mickey Lewis would *definitely* have been there!'

* * *

The fact of it being the playing season clearly never stopped Mickey and his crew. But as a collective, they found another gear once the close season came round. And they often did so in sunnier climes. The trip to Spain on which Mickey threw Heath and his plaster cast into the sea being a classic example.

Mickey was organiser and ringleader. He always was. Yet even with this administrative responsibility, Heath remembers how Mickey arrived at Heathrow, saddling up to the group with just a single Tesco carrier bag. 'Where's your stuff, Mick? Where are your clothes?'

Mickey had decided he didn't need such luxuries. He had the shorts and socks he was wearing, a couple of pairs of pants and a toothbrush.

'What are you going to wear, Mick?' It was team-mate Dave Penney who asked the sensible question.

'Well, Dave, I'm going to wear your clothes,' Mickey answered with a chuckle.

A week into the trip and with only a couple of pairs of underwear left, Penney took a stroll down to Puerto Banús after a heavy day of drinking. He approached a roundabout with a large fountain in the middle.

'Who's that idiot in the fountain?' Penney's thought was a fair one. 'He's going to get arrested if he isn't careful.'

Oh, wait. 'That's my shirt,' Penney thought. He soon realised that the soon-to-be-criminal in question had all of Penney's clothes on.

It was Mickey. Just cooling down before dinner.

In all this, Heath was quick to stress Mickey never got in any trouble or any fights. Heath echoed many others on that point: a total troublemaker, never in any trouble.

But even once Penney had encouraged Mickey out of the fountain, there was no let-up. In fact, groundsman Mick Moore remembers one of the later afternoons on the trip, in which

Mickey was clearly up for what Moore described as 'some kind of bender'.

As a responsible, slightly older member of the clan, Moore was wary to avoid whatever was planned.

So as the squad was heading out to town, Moore took a different route and had a late lunch on his own. He made his way back to the hotel in peace. In peace, that is, until he heard a ruckus from one of the other rooms. He couldn't help but pop his head in to see what was happening.

'Come on Mooresy, have a drink with us!'

The big smile and open arms came, as they so often did, from Mickey.

'They were on the sangria,' Moore told us. 'Mickey said "Have some of this." I told them I shouldn't. He said "Come on, just one, it can't hurt – this is the 16th jug we've had today!"'

* * *

So, it seems Mickey liked few things more than settling in with team-mates, friends and family for a jug (or 16!) of sangria at a table in the European sun. Or waiting for the heat to go out of the day, at which point the group could transfer to the karaoke bar, where he could take up his regular slot and deliver his interpretation of Lionel Richie's 'All Night Long' or his favourite, Frank Sinatra's 'My Way'.

That was the attitude with which Mickey lived. If you go into anything with the intention of having a good time and not taking life or yourself too seriously, if you're good to people and good to be around, things will work themselves out just fine.

201

He was, really, just the sort of person that everyone wanted to be around. As Craig Adey described, he was 'the centre of the room without wanting to be, [he'd] just make you feel comfortable'. For Heath, 'Mickey was just the best laugh.' He enjoyed the occasion and, because of that, everyone else did, too.

Chapter 23

Time to slow down?

DID THINGS change when Mickey became a coach? Not a chance.

John Clinkard was the Oxford United physio throughout Mickey's time as a player there. And he was quick to stress that Mickey never took himself too seriously, even when he took on the additional responsibility that comes with moving from the pitch to the dugout. And there was one particular story that Clinkard was keen to tell to make that point.

It was early January in 2000 and Oxford United were playing away at Cardiff City. It was not an easy moment for Mickey – who was in temporary charge at 34 – or the club. An unbeaten run through the autumn was over and Oxford were in the middle of what would be a run of one point from six matches. As Clinkard put it, they were 'scratching for results'. The much-loved kitman, Ken Ridley, was taken ill with an acute case of angina in the first half of the game and he was driven straight to Cardiff Royal Infirmary. Upon hearing after the game that Ridley would be kept in overnight, Clinkard and Mickey stopped off at the hospital before heading back to Cardiff Central railway station. But they couldn't see a train to London on the board when they arrived at the station. They asked a steward, who informed them that the last train back to London was long gone. Oops.

The steward suggested they could get a three-hour train to Birmingham and jump on a train to London from there. Mickey loved the idea, but said there was no need for the second leg, since his mum lived in Birmingham and they could just stay there.

'Most managers of a professional club wouldn't have done that,' Clinkard suggests. 'They'd have said, "Right, we're getting a taxi, charging it to the club and getting back as quickly as possible."'

Instead, this minor crisis turned into one of Clinkard's fondest memories of Mickey.

'It's a Saturday night. You're up for a pint. We sunk a couple on the train and got to Mickey's mum's house. She made us the nicest bacon and eggs ever. We had four cans of beer each and slept together in the same double bed. It was like we were kids again.'

And so, Oxford United's caretaker manager and physio got back home on Sunday afternoon with a minor hangover and a story to tell.

Clinkard had to explain to his wife what had happened and why he hadn't come home the night before. We suggested she might have thought he was up to no good in Cardiff, to which Clinkard responded:

'Well, she's my ex-wife now!'

* * *

That minor Cardiff to Birmingham adventure wasn't an isolated incident. It wasn't part of an adjustment period as Mickey made the transition from player to coach, getting some final bits of mischief out of his system as he did so. The mischief kept coming at pace.

Take, for example, Mickey's approach to his work at Oxford City, also in the early 2000s.

The club had a steward at the time who used to take on the additional tasks of washing the kit and looking after the balls. He also often told those who would listen in Marsh Lane's front row that he used to play a lot of football before his knees gave in.

Word had filtered back to Mickey, who was amused by this misguided case of self-promotion. So, there was Mickey and Oxford City's Paul Lee having a pint of Guinness and some pork scratchings in the City bar, as the double doors swung open. The steward walked in with a ball at his feet. He'd come to deliver some kit, have a laugh with the gaffer and leave with a pat on the back.

Mickey turned to Lee and chuckled. Lee knew what was coming. That's the power of a strong personality – you learn to see the punchlines ahead of time.

Mickey set his beer down, hopped down from the barstool and charged at the self-proclaimed midfield maestro. Two seconds later, the folded kits were scattered across the room and the steward was staring up at Mickey's curly hair and curvy smile. 'Mad Dog' had planted a two-footed, socks-up (no shoes in the clubhouse) tackle on him to the delight of those who had stayed for one extra pint.

Lee recalled the moment fondly: 'The steward had clearly never played the game in his life. Mickey frightened him to death!'

But surely he was angry at Mickey? A natural question, we thought. Surely the 'Mad Dog' took it too far on occasions? 'Oh no. No, no, no. Never. No one was ever angry at Mad Dog. That steward enjoyed being upended by him.'

Enjoyed getting flattened by a two-footer on a felt carpet at nine o'clock on a Tuesday? That's charisma, right?

* * *

Those who know Chris Wilder may assume that Mickey might finally have mellowed once Wilder had arrived to take Oxford United's top job. But they'd be wrong again.

Now, Wilder is a serious man. He has spent his career doing serious jobs. None more so than the job he is once more doing, at the time of writing, trying to return Sheffield United to the Premier League at the first time of asking, with the task's seismic financial stakes and the far-reaching implications, not just for the club but for the community and the city. He's surely a man who prizes the precious 15 minutes of an in-game half-time, those 15 minutes in which managers work desperately to earn their keep, lift chins and get football matches won.

By his own admission, though, that has not always been the case. When Mickey was part of the equation, things were a little different.

Wilder remembers one particularly high stakes match on Oxford's journey back into the Football League, shortly before their big day at Wembley in 2010. There was a bumper crowd and Setanta was at the ground to broadcast live, which was no small deal for Wilder, Mickey and the managerial team as they worked to build their reputation in the game. But whilst the managerial team was surely focused on the task at hand, Mickey's eye wandered for a moment to the beer fridge in the manager's office.

The fridge was usually well-stocked, ready for the post-match drink with the opposing manager. A rare moment in a tough and sometimes lonely role to reflect on and dissect the 90 minutes. Or, perhaps, a chance to rant and rave about the referee without the threat of an FA fine.

Instead, Mickey noticed that the fridge was empty, which was perhaps reflective of the state of the club's finances at the time. And so, Mickey rang wife Suzanne in a panic, with a plea to bring a box of beer to the changing room as quickly as possible.

By half-time things were going well for Oxford, having scored twice without reply. Oxford's players might well have been expecting the coaching staff's reflections on the half of football they'd just played. They might have been hoping for a pat on the back, having executed the game plan well.

In the manager's office, though, attention was elsewhere. The box of beers had arrived. That part had gone to plan. But the beers weren't fitting in the fridge. Mickey was on the floor, hunched over the fridge, cursing loudly as he failed to solve the complexities of the bottle–fridge conundrum. As Wilder remembers: 'There were beers spinning all over the place, bottles flying out of the fridge.'

As Wilder reflects now: 'What the hell were we doing? I guess it was a good job we won.'

It is a memory reflective of a different era, but also Mickey's relentless ability to find humour and fun in the unlikeliest, most pressured situations.

And whilst he didn't make a habit of celebrating 2-0 half-time leads, he did make sure the fridge was always stocked.

* * *

Dan Bond was barely out of university when he joined Mickey and Wilder on the Oxford United staff. Bond would travel with the staff to every away match, so spent every other Friday night, once the players had gone up to their rooms, getting 'fucking steaming in the hotel lobby'. Bond had been part of his university football club and was no stranger to a drinking culture. But he had never seen anything like it. Such was the ferocity and velocity with which the staff worked through the pints, Bond mused whether 'nowadays it would be deemed dangerous'.What Bond remembers just as much as the Friday night drinking, though, are the Saturday mornings in the hotel gym. 'Mickey would always be sitting there on the bike, going hell for leather.' From what he'd learned on his sports science degree, Bond recognised that Mickey was pushing close to his maximum heart rate, for 35 to 40 minutes at a time, with the resistance almost as high as it could go. He was 'fucking breathing and snotting everywhere'.

All the while, instead of water, Mickey would have a cup of hot tea. He had to burn the alcohol off somehow. As Oxford captain and Wembley goalscorer James Constable remembers it, even when you'd heard Mickey and the staff coming back in the early hours 'he knew he had a responsibility'.

So, in the space of a few hours each weekend, Bond was learning up close what it meant to work hard, play hard. To play the game but to enjoy the occasion, too.

Chapter 24

The 19th hole

IT IS only recently that England's top clubs have started enjoying annual pre-season jaunts traversing the coasts and commercial interests of their American fans and investors or brand-building across Asia's great cities and centres of enthusiastic football populations. Clubs have only recently fallen into the habit of placating tricky sponsors with trips to the United Arab Emirates or Saudi Arabia. Players have only recently started organising extravagant close season trips to Las Vegas or to the most expensive golf courses in some of the most exclusive corners of the Algarve.

But Mickey had shown during his time as a player that he'd enjoyed time in the sun whenever the opportunity had presented itself in the close season. So, as he transitioned away from playing, he was not about to let the small matter of retirement and his new-found coaching responsibilities disrupt his commitment to enjoying the occasion on an international away day.

* * *

Part of Mickey's responsibilities to the Oxford college programme on which he coached in the early 2000s – and during which he met Oxford United's current and prodigiously talented manager Des Buckingham – was to take the players on an end-of-season tour.

And Buckingham's memories of their shared trip to Salou in Spain – on which he wryly recalled they were '*supposed* to compete in a football tournament' – were primarily memories of time spent with and learning from one of the tour's 'responsible adults'.

Things started with the mid-afternoon hotel arrival, at which point Mickey was soon teaching the touring party drinking games and setting out the misdemeanours that would constitute a fine across the week. Buckingham remembers that one such misdemeanour was the small act of having a post-match shower: 'We had lads literally using soap as hair gel.'

As the squad readied themselves for the first night of the tour, Mickey convinced Andy Slater – the man in charge of the trip – to let him take the squad out into central Salou. Slater acquiesced and, as midnight came and went, Mickey led the charge out to the nearby bars.

One curious observer from another of the competing colleges was incredulous. He asked Buckingham how they were being allowed out so late and where exactly the responsible adult was. 'Well,' Buckingham replied, 'he's at the front of the conga line.'

Now, whilst much of the above wouldn't get past even the lightest-touch pre-tour risk assessments today, we would stress that Mickey wasn't being irresponsible. In fact, whether intentionally or not, we would suggest he was teaching the young men in his charge some quite fundamental skills for life beyond football.

As Buckingham explained: 'His one rule was that if you see your friend in trouble then you get them home, and those who asked for the taxi money got it. Though, of course, you got yourself back out there after.'

As for the football? All you need to know about the relative importance of the tournament was that Mickey sent the team out on to the pitch with a two euro coin and three rules. The first rule: you can't refuse the coin if someone hands it to you during the game. Second: you can't hand the coin back to the person who's just given it to you. Third: the person with the coin at the end of the match was the one responsible for the first round at the post-match bar.

It's perhaps unsurprising then that Buckingham claims he can't remember any of the results from the tour. He does, however, remember Mickey being up on the table in one of the Salou bars, powering through his version of 'Bohemian Rhapsody'. 'The owner was going absolutely nuts, telling him that should be one of the players, not the coach!'

Such was the impression that Mickey's performance left, Buckingham and his long-standing friends from the programme continued to leave a voicemail on Mickey's phone in the early hours of the morning whenever they heard the song in a club or bar.

* * *

The small matter of being responsible for a professional football team didn't change Mickey's approach to opportunities for pre- or post-season excitement.

He often took the squad down to HMS *Collingwood* on pre-season training camps, facilitated by Ian Matthews. And Matthews remembers Mickey and the staff making full use of the mess and its subsidised pricing.

Mark Edwards of the *Oxford Mail* remembered Oxford United's pre-season trip to Scotland in a similar vein, as his 'favourite-slash-worst story about Mickey'.

Edwards joined Mickey, the United staff and the playing squad for their pre-season tour to Scotland. The brief he received from his employers at the *Oxford Mail* was clear: report on the tour in 'as few nights as possible and use the cheapest accommodation possible'. From the club? Well, 'yes, but we'll need a bit of distance from you, don't report *everything* that happens'. Maybe the press office had heard about the legend of the cowboys and Indians.

With the parameters more or less established and the cost of a flight out of the question, Edwards was out of the house in the early hours of a late summer Saturday morning to begin his long drive up to Greenock Morton for the first match. The match itself was, as far as Edwards remembers, a bog standard pre-season affair. By the final whistle, he was shattered, ready to retire to his *Mail*-approved hotel to file his copy and get to bed.

This is where Mickey comes into the story. He, of course, had other ideas: 'Mark, can you do me a favour? We've only got two mini buses and we've got all the staff and the players and the equipment. Could you take one of the trialists back to the hotel?'

Edwards obliged. But by the time of the drop-off, Mickey had his teeth in. He was raring to go. And he wasn't about to let Edwards off the hook: 'Right, cheers Mark. Just to let you know, in half an hour I'll need you to be here at our hotel.'

Once Edwards had slipped away back to his hotel, loosely promising Mickey he'd see him again that evening, the early start, hundreds of miles on the road and 200-calorie lunch got the better of him. Delaying the piece he needed to write until the morning, he swiftly fell asleep.

Of course, you know what happens next.

The sleep was soon disturbed.

First, Mickey phoned. 'Mark, where are you? Get yourself here. We're waiting.' The clink of glasses was no doubt audible in the background. More loose promises and, again, the swift drift back to sleep.

Then, a banging at the door.

Mickey had taken matters into his own hands. He waited for Edwards to change, walked him back to the squad's hotel and straight into the bar, lined him up three catch-up beers and once those beer glasses were totally dry, got the night on its way.

Now, Edwards remembers nothing after 11pm. He woke up at 2pm the next day to a long-passed deadline and several missed calls from his boss.

Naturally, that was not the point of the memory for Edwards:

'Mickey didn't need to do that. Nobody else there was fussed either way. Most of them probably would have preferred for me not to be there, but that wasn't Mickey. As far as he was concerned, I was up there, I was part of the group. That was Mickey through and through.'

* * *

By 2012, the club had traded Scotland for the east coast of America and Greenock Morton for Seacoast United. The change of backdrop did little to dull Mickey's appetite for adventure.

This time, it was David Pritchard's turn to join the group on behalf of the city's local press corps. Chris Williams, from the club's in-house communications team, was there, too.

Pritchard particularly remembers the tour's rest day. Oxford's Seacoast hosts laid on a golf day at the impressive Granite Fields in New Hampshire. The format was a shotgun start – meaning everyone starts at the same time, just from different holes – so all players and hosts could finish at the same time for the prize presentation and the barbecue.

As Williams tells it: 'No one could believe that people would pay money to play golf with us.' And as the players and staff milled around the club before the round, the excitement was all too much for some members of the travelling party. Mickey was, by all accounts, totally giddy as the groups headed out on their well-stocked buggies for the day. And as dusk fell over the course and the round was drawing to a close, it became clear one party was missing. 'Has anybody seen Mick?'

Mickey had gone out with his coaching counterpart, Andy Melville. A middle-aged American couple – likely some sort of Seacoast superfans or sponsors – had the honour of filling out the fourball.

On Pritchard's retelling, Mickey and Melville had soon realised Granite Fields was a hospitable course. So much so, in fact, that you could order beers straight to your buggy. The woman responsible for the cart service was called Kelly Kelly. Or so Williams told us, at least. And Mickey's group became well acquainted with Ms Kelly, after Mickey introduced a playing rule in which none of the four – including the kindly American couple – could tee off unless they had an open bottle of Budweiser on the tee box with them.

As the light faded, the group had, as Pritchard politely put it, 'played the 19th hole a few more times than any of the other 18'. So, it was not until an hour and a half after all the other groups had finished that Mickey and his playing partners finally rolled into the clubhouse. The barbecue was long finished. The presentation was done.

You have to wonder what the Americans thought. But Mickey's ability to enjoy an occasion was matched only by his ability to find the right words at the right time. As he joined up with the rest of the group, he turned to his team-mates, grinning from ear to ear: 'I don't think we'd have won anything anyway.'

Chapter 25

'You can't sledge a 14-year-old boy'

SO, MICKEY enjoyed the occasion at every available opportunity, even as his playing days faded further into the rear-view mirror.

There are few greater opportunities for revelry than a wedding day. But just to raise the stakes a little further, in late 2004, Mickey and Suzanne celebrated their wedding, only to host a joint birthday party two months later in early 2005.

The proximity of the two events remains the source of some confusion for those who attended both. And several guests remember one particular story – the stuff of legend amongst Mickey and Suzanne's friends – as having happened at Mickey and Suzanne's wedding. But Suzanne confirms it actually happened at the party.

Hazy memories aside, we like to think of this story as Mickey's version of the Sir Alex Ferguson–David Beckham shoegate. The one where Fergie kicked a boot across the dressing room and it struck Becks above the eye, causing an injury that – at least allegedly – required stitches. Though the incident at

Mickey and Suzanne's birthday party obviously caused less of a national uproar.

As Mickey's best man, Phil Heath, talked us through what happened, he couldn't help but chuckle to himself, as people do when recalling their fondest memories. The party was in full swing. Top buttons were undone, ties were loose and heels had been changed to dancing pumps. The DJ reached for Frank Sinatra, as Mickey would have insisted on. The crowd dived into 'New York, New York', with Mickey right there in the centre belting out the chorus and pulling out the highest leg lifts he and his tight hamstrings could manage.

Until, that is, his shoe came off, flew across the dancefloor and struck an unsuspecting partygoer. 'It was surely about 40 miles per hour,' Heath suggested with only a slight note of exaggeration.

Heath remembers the unlucky victim as being the Oxford United coach driver. He recalls a split forehead and four or five stitches, though the need for first aid is disputed by others. Paul Lee told us separately that the shoe actually hit the goalkeeper, Phil Whitehead. In Lee's telling, Whitehead – he of hundreds of professional games for Oxford and West Brom – tried to catch the shoe, failed and ended the evening drinking through a straw after it hit him in the mouth. We've also heard a version where the shoe hits a waiter.

We think the fact we heard such different versions of this story tells you everything you need to know about the party.

It was clearly a party that would have needed more than a flying shoe to bring things to a standstill. Just ask

Des Buckingham. He was 19 at the time and, as he put it, he 'got talking to this young lady, Jemma, at the bar and she asked me what I did. I told her I was a football player for Reading.'

That little white lie – a lie that promoted Buckingham into a Reading first team for which he'd never played – might have been the end of it. But Buckingham hadn't reckoned on Mickey Lewis.

'I was skulking out and there was Mick and Suzy, they'd got the guy behind the bar to keep serving them. And sitting with them was Jemma from the bar. She says, "That's who I was talking about earlier, the Reading player"'. Cue uproarious laughter. And, naturally, Mickey made sure Buckingham was suitably embarrassed, as well as never letting him forget that evening. Though Buckingham was quick to add that he and Jemma are now firm friends.

* * *

If Saturday evenings were for parties, karaoke and shoeless sliding tackles, Sundays were so often for cricket. Several members of Mickey's extended family had been passionate cricket fans, enjoying playing and watching it even more so than they did football. So, it was natural for Mickey, who showed as instinctive an aptitude for cricket as he did all sports, to go in search of a game the afternoon after the night before.

Kelvin Thomas was especially excited to talk about his and Mickey's Sunday cricket team, which they filled out with an assortment of players, coaches and friends who were around in the close4 season. They would regularly end up playing village and wandering sides across the Oxfordshire area. Mickey would captain the side and keep wicket, and Mark Edwards recalls a flamboyance with bat in hand, too. Thomas would usually keep Mickey company from first slip.

As Thomas remembers it, Mickey split his time behind the wicket into two key tasks. The first: protecting the beer that he'd always have tucked behind the stumps. The second: relentlessly sledging the batsman. 'Mick, the boy's 14,' Thomas would sometimes say. 'You can't sledge a 14-year-old boy.'

Of course, he could and, of course, he did. And we're sure Mickey would have done it in a way that guaranteed the young lad enjoyed the joshing. That's who Mickey was.

* * *

So, Mickey Lewis played the game, but he enjoyed the occasion, too.

He was a man who had what many described as an incredible and rare appetite for life. He was, as Phil Heath described him, a man who only needed two playing cards to invent a card game. Or a football and a wall. If he had a co-conspirator, all the better. And with this appetite and his commitment to enjoying whatever occasion he found himself in, he was a man who usually found himself surrounded by good people, too.

As Jim Magilton remembered:

'Mickey was always my barometer in life, in terms of people in football. If Mickey didn't like someone, it meant they weren't worth spending much time with. Mickey liked most people, so if Mickey didn't like you, I always felt there was a reason for that. He was always on the money.'

What does all this mean? What impact did his passion for mischief and revelry, as well as good experiences in good company, have on the people around him? At the end of each interview, we asked Mickey's friends and family exactly that. And it was his Oxford United team-mate Andy Melville who perhaps said it best: 'Thank you for the time we had together, for the guidance, for the education. Oh, and thanks for plenty of hangovers.'

Would Mickey have thrived quite as much in a post-Wenger, post-sports science era, once the pints of Guinness had been replaced by the isotonic drinks and twice-daily yoga? Well, we'll leave that one up to you.

But what is sure is that Mickey's approach provides a blueprint for how to get the most out of work and life. Though we certainly wouldn't recommend 16 jugs of sangria or hosting a cowboys and Indians party in an Oxford pub – both might end up getting you arrested – there is something profound in Mickey's commitment to celebrating the ups and downs, personal and professional, as they happened.

It was how he took the pressure off, emphasised enjoyment, got the best out of himself and those around him, and ultimately guaranteed the best possible performance. It was the way in which he demonstrated that, whilst the result surely matters, it's the memories of the experiences and the occasions that last far longer and ultimately matter more.

SECTION FOUR:

ONE FOR THE ROAD

Mickey transitioned from the first team on to the club's staff in 1996, initially to work with the club's youth team. He was only 31, though his combative playing style was unforgiving for his own body, as well as for others.

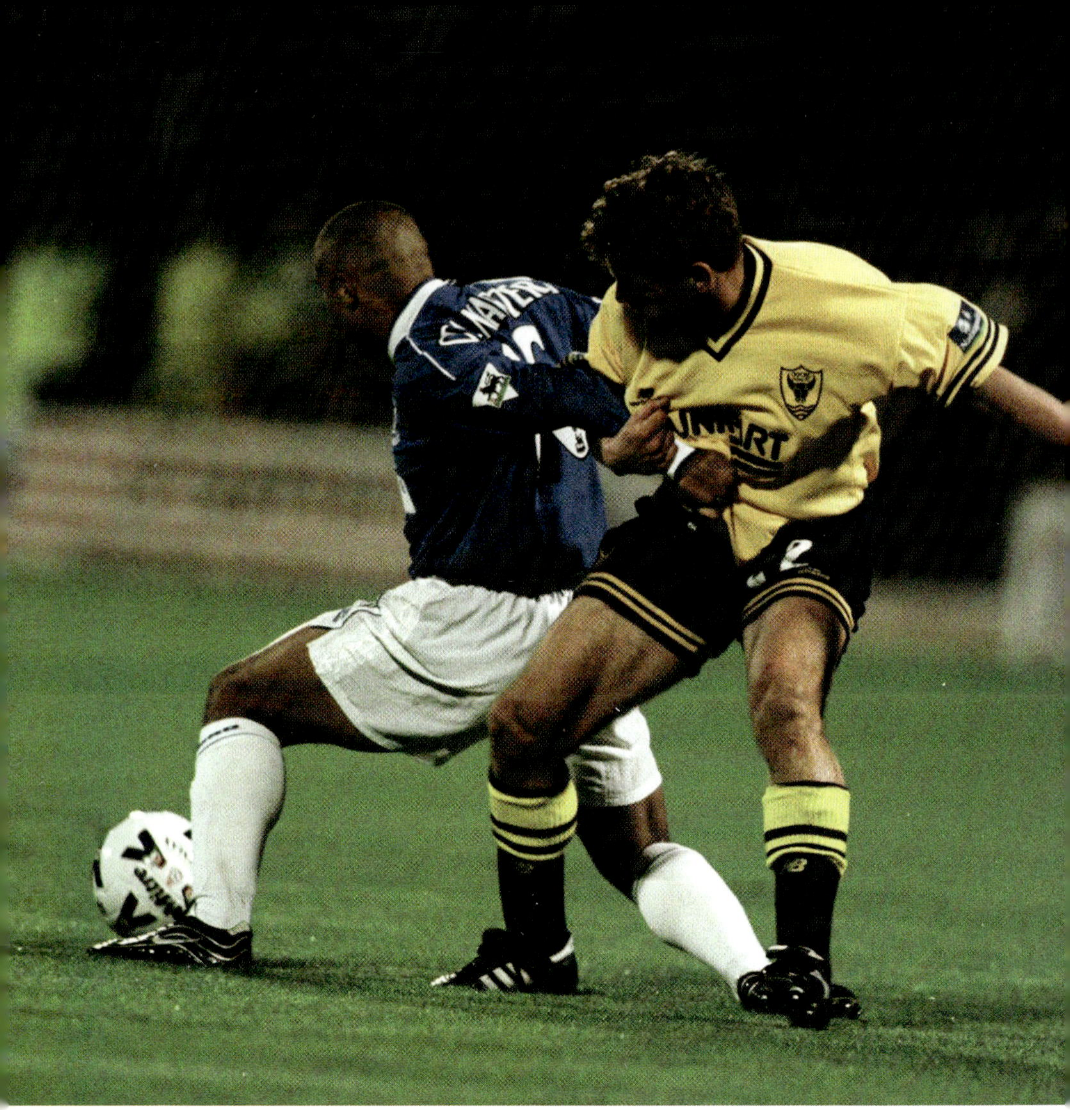

Mickey first tried to retire from playing in 1996, aged 31. But with Oxford in the grip of an injury crisis, he returned to give a career best performance in the League Cup giant-killing of Everton, in September 1999.

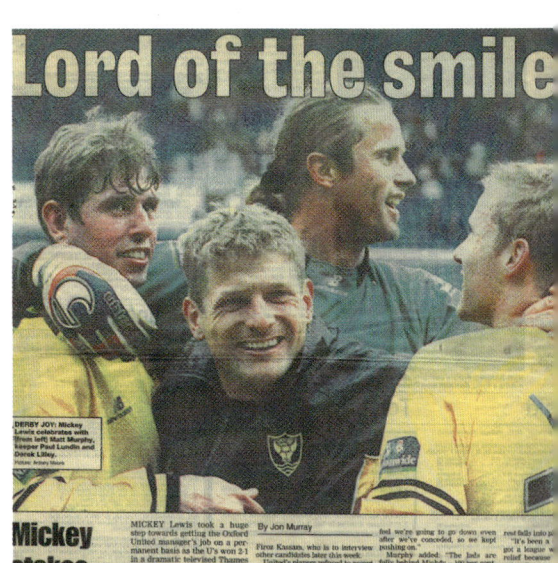

Lord of the smile

DERBY JOY: Mickey Lewis celebrates with (from left) Matt Murphy, keeper Paul Lundin and Derek Lilley.

Picture: Antony Moore

Mickey stakes top job claim

By Jon Murray

MICKEY Lewis took a huge step towards getting the Oxford United manager's job on a permanent basis as the U's won 2-1 in a dramatic televised Thames Valley derby at Reading.

A spectacular late winner from Matt Murphy gave United their first Division 2 win since beating Bristol City in September.

Yet it was the manner of the performance, with Oxford's players clearly showing how much they wanted to get a victory for the caretaker boss, which will have

Firoz Kassam, who is to interview other candidates later this week.

United's players refused to accept a draw after Reading levelled late in the game, and that single-minded determination helped bring Murphy his chance, which the midfielder buried for one of the best goals he's ever scored.

"Not many of them go in like that, so I'll be keeping the video," said Murphy as he reflected on his ninth goal of the season.

feel we're going to go down even after we've conceded, so we kept pushing on."

Murphy added: "The lads are fully behind Micky – 100 per cent. There's no-one who would not want Mickey in charge.

"I know there's a few who are not going to be happy because they're not in the team, but generally, everyone's really happy about Mickey being there.

"Whether that's going to be the case is not in our hands, but we can try and do it on the pitch and push

rest falls into p

"It's been a got a league w relief because points."

Lewis himse was a fantastic brilliant da involved," he sa

"We were un defended brill great character

An away wi

Mickey's first spell as caretaker manager at his beloved Oxford United couldn't have started better. He was every bit the 'Lord of the Smiles'. Unfortunately, results soon turned.

By late 1999, Mickey's playing career was over and his first experience of first team management had begun. He was still only 34.

Just as Mickey had established himself as a fixture of the Oxford United midfield, he was soon a fixture of the club's staff, doing everything from driving the bus to stepping in as physio. He had a particularly significant impact on a certain Des Buckingham, on the right here.

As a player and then as a coach, no matter what was happening on the pitch or in the dugout, no job was too small or menial for Mickey.

When he left Oxford United in 2000, Mickey built a portfolio of coaching work in the Oxford area. And he was soon describing his work with the University of Oxford first team, or the 'Blues', as some of the happiest of his career. Even if the stadiums were a little emptier than he was used to.

The University of Oxford team might have been some way from the professional game in which Mickey had made his name, but he knew how much it meant to the players, and so he cared deeply too.

Mickey's approach to life was quite simple – work hard, but enjoy the occasion when you can, too. Here he is with the Varsity trophy, on one of the many occasions he masterminded an Oxford win in the historic fixture.

The Oxford United 'Legends Team' had an impressive roster for Mickey's 'One for the Road' memorial match, which took place at the Kassam Stadium in October 2021. Not least with Jim Magilton in midfield and Steve McClaren on the touchline.

Mickey returned for another spell at Oxford United. After Chris Wilder's appointment in 2008, the pair were inseparable, in the dugout and away from the pitch. They remained close friends until Mickey's passing, and Wilder still hosts Mickey's son Zach at Sheffield United games, though Zach's allegiances are split between multiple teams.

Mickey's son Zach, in the dark blue of the University of Oxford side, scored a hat-trick at the 'One for the Road' memorial match.

■ PLOTTING: Oxford United's management team of Chris Wilder, Mickey and Andy Melville deep in conversation when the U's travelled to Wycombe in the season, have challenged the team to deliver the goods today.

Oxford United's win at Wembley, in the 2010 Conference play-off final, was one of Mickey's favourite days in football. He celebrated it with some of his closest friends on the pitch, and then for a few more days after that.

A minute of silence at the Kassam Stadium on 6 March 2021, the day after Mickey tragically passed away, aged just 56.

The University of Oxford fielded the youngest of the four teams for Mickey's 'One for the Road' memorial. Leo Ackerman, this book's co-author, is three in from the right on the back row.

When Chris Wilder left Oxford, his trajectory certainly differed from Mickey's. But that didn't stop Mickey inspiring hundreds if not thousands of young players – and we think that is central to understanding his legacy.

Keep playing. You really can't beat it.

Chapter 26

Hat-trick for Lewis!

'There is real pride, knowing that we had the
chance to have him in our lives. We're still
incredibly grateful that we had time with him.'

Paul Charles, chairman of Stonesfield Strikers

AS 2020 became 2021 and the country continued to grapple
with the realities of the pandemic, Mickey, like so many
others involved in sport, was enduring a stop-start period of
his coaching career. Where the Covid rules allowed, he was
on training pitches across Oxfordshire, from the university to
Oxford City and Stonesfield Strikers.

But, of course, our introduction to Mickey's story started
at his memorial match. And it was a memorial match that took
place because, tragically, Mickey died on 5 March 2021. He had
just turned 56 years old. He was survived by his wife, Suzanne,
and his son, Zach, who was eight.

Everything happened quickly.

Phil Heath remembers seeing Mickey on New Year's Day to exchange presents. They did so on the doorstep, as the rules of the third national lockdown dictated. He was bundling around as ever, rushing off to the shops, promising a video call in the coming days.

When Heath went round to drop off another present in mid-February – this time for Mickey's birthday – there was no doorstep conversation. Mickey texted to say he was unwell and couldn't come down. Heath remembers thinking this was unusual. But this was in the middle of the third national lockdown in England, illness was everywhere, and so, naturally, Heath assumed Mickey would soon be better.

But Mickey's illness persisted and worsened. So he went to the hospital. Soon after he was diagnosed with a rare, aggressive lung cancer. The doctor gave him little time to live.

Those closest to him were kind enough to share with us their memories of the time. The conversations were raw and emotional, reflective of the fact that for both us and those we interviewed, what happened becomes no less tragic, or sad, with the passage of time.

How was Mickey through all this? Well, whilst the lockdown and the severity of his illness limited his ability to see anyone beyond his closest family, he was still active on his phone, responding to the supportive texts that came in as a deluge from the moment the news began to spread.

Close friend and former colleague Kelvin Thomas was one of those in closest touch with Mickey until the end. He sent Mickey a zip-up top from Northampton Town, the club he now runs. It was something that was easy to take on and off. And he sent him a club link to watch a match that Northampton were playing. 'He was typical Mickey, trying to be upbeat, texting about the game, even though he was really struggling. And all the while he was trying to make sure other people, Suzy, Zach, were okay.'

Mickey's partner-in-crime from his time at Hayes & Yeading and the Reading academy, Tristan Lewis, said something similar. Tristan was clearly emotional as he talked about his wife, who runs a league in Oxford in which Mickey was involved, sending an administrative request around the time Mickey was in hospital. 'He still responded, for the boys,' Tristan remembers, 'so they could play.' And at the same time, Mickey was talking to Stonesfield's Paul Charles about home training videos for their young players, as they navigated another Covid break in their own fledgling football careers.

Mickey's modesty and humility was defining to the end. As Oxford City's Paul Lee told us, 'He was clearly in a lot of pain,' but he was bashful about the attention. 'He was apologising. That sort of thing sums him up. He had nothing to apologise for.'

Of course, it is a natural human reaction, even in the face of all the evidence, to hold out hope for a miracle. As Mickey's friend and Doncaster colleague Dave Penney described: 'Everyone thought Mickey was indestructible. He was never ill, he never missed games, never missed training.'

It is understandable then that the news of Mickey's passing, when it came, was still a wrenching shock.

Even the notoriously cool Chris Wilder was unusually emotional as he reflected on what happened, pausing for a moment or two as we spoke on the phone. 'The speed of it all just took everybody aback. It was head-scratching, staggering, heartbreaking. I get it, tragic things happen. But the way it happened, how quickly it happened, it was staggering and so, so sad.'

For Thomas, who was in Florida at the time, 'I spoke to Chris [Wilder], I spoke to Mary [Page] and then the only thing I could do was what Mickey would have expected – have one for the road.'

This was a phrase that followed and continues to follow Mickey everywhere: 'One for the road.' They were the four words he would excitedly say, usually preceded by a chirpy 'come on, mate', whenever a friend, team-mate, family member or fan was considering leaving the pub for an early night. Mickey would, several interviewees told us, sidle over, swing his arm around your shoulder and tell you that you had one more in you. 'I'll get it for ya, don't worry.' Mickey would bring another round in and you'd be happily lost in conversation with him until the barman decided it was bedtime.

It was the phrase that so many came to associate with Mickey's sense of humour, his love for a good conversation and his philosophy of always living for others. Many of those who were close to Mickey now have a bottle opener with the phrase engraved on it, in his memory. And when we asked friends of Mickey what they would say to him given the chance, it wasn't just Thomas who reached for the poignant phrase.

* * *

It's clear that Mickey Lewis had an outsized and profound impact on hundreds if not thousands of lives. Old team-mates and friends reflected on this period through tears, tracing aloud the thread from their time on the training ground or in the bar with Mickey through to how they thought about and approached life today. Or telling us how their son's middle name was Lewis.

And nowhere was this clearer than in the tributes that followed the announcement of Mickey's death. They were countless. National and local news ran obituaries, with much of Oxford in mourning. Social media and fansites were flooded with videos of Mickey's (handful of) goals and his (plentiful) thunderous tackles, memories of his best performances and anecdotes about the man behind the 'Mad Dog'. Players from every period of Mickey's life mobilised through WhatsApp groups to share stories and talk about honouring Mickey's legacy. Hundreds of people contributed to fundraisers too.

In all this, there were stories about nights on the training pitch trying desperately to avoid his nutmeg or trying and failing to trap him in the centre of a keep-ball circle. There were players who'd moved on to new challenges as under-nines football coaches, joking that they couldn't wait until they, too, could get their kids turning and getting the ball into the channels. Teachers talked about walking into difficult situations in the classroom while thinking to themselves, 'What would Mickey do?' Men well into their professional lives wanted to tell Mickey that they still thought about his changing-room adages and that they walked into job interviews with his voice in their head, telling them to not let it pass them by. Dads with babies in their arms chuckled as they reminisced on Mickey's hobbling knees and told him that he had inspired them to be a better father.

* * *

Given the number of people wanting to pay their respects to a man who'd shaped their lives in such a lasting way, it is a great sadness that the funeral was subject to the Covid restrictions still blighting those wanting to celebrate and mourn up and down the country.

We watched via the video link. One of us in a quiet corner at work in London and another on his sofa from Switzerland.

We watched as crowds gathered at Oxford City and lined the streets on the route to the service. Chris Wilder and Kelvin Thomas joined Mickey's closest friends and extended family. The entrance music was 'Abide With Me'. A poem asked 'What Is Success?' Suzanne delivered the eulogy and then Ben Putland, who had captained Mickey's final university squad, delivered a moving tribute on behalf of the club for whom Mickey had become such a central part and a club which had become so central for Mickey, too. That tribute is included in full at the back of this book.

Those present were then asked to think on their reflections of Mickey whilst listening to Mickey's favourite song, 'My Way'.

And all the while, Mickey's son, Zach, sat quietly in the front row.

It was profoundly moving, even before the service played out the only way it possibly could, with the unerringly positive and forward-looking hymn 'One More Step Along the World I Go'.

* * *

And so, we come back to Oxford, on Sunday, 10 October 2021, when thousands of fans, friends and family descended upon Oxford United's Kassam Stadium to pay tribute to Mickey 'Mad Dog' Lewis.

Discussions took place at Oxford United on what the event should be called. It didn't take long to figure out. The day would be advertised under a simple banner: Mickey Lewis: One for the Road.

And as captured in the prologue, it was a special day. A day of reunions, of full-blooded football, of a celebration of life that stretched deep into the night. It was a day that led one of the university footballers to conclude that 'there was a bit of Mickey Lewis in that'. And as Oxford journalist Mark Edwards put it: 'Days like that don't just happen for anyone, you know.'

Now, what would Mickey have thought of all the tributes and the emotion?

For a man who went through his life avoiding fuss and recognition, perhaps he would have rolled his eyes at all the attention. That was certainly the view of Jim Rosenthal, who knew Mickey well throughout their respective associations with Oxford United: 'Mickey would have been embarrassed by the tributes. He was never one to bask in a personal spotlight.'

But, of course, he'd have dived into the action, too. Phil Heath imagined he'd have been out there in the middle of the match between the university side and the United veterans, putting a few tackles in, making sure things stayed competitive. Kelvin Thomas thought similarly: 'He'd have loved the day, being in the changing room with all the guys. He'd have been right amongst it.'

Above all, he'd have loved how much of the day was focused on his son, Zach.

From the moment Zach was born, he was the centre of Mickey's life. Chris Wilder recalls evenings out with the two families during which, the moment Mickey and Zach spotted a strip of grass, they'd be off with a football, Mickey charging around at full pelt and full stretch, usually with a beer going warm, forgotten, back at the table. And it wasn't like Mickey to leave a pint undrunk.

That is why so many of those present at the Kassam treasure the memory of Zach bursting through on goal and scoring in front of thousands at the Kassam. A memory amongst many that, despite the profoundly difficult backdrop, Zach will hopefully treasure for a long time, too.

And Kelvin Thomas ensures Zach is now a regular in the boardroom at Northampton. In fact, if you bump into him on a Saturday, he'll be keeping track of at least five different football scores – Thomas's Northampton, Buckingham's Oxford United, Wilder's Sheffield United, Oxford City and the university – such is the protective circle that's been wrapped around him by Mickey's friends and team-mates across football.

* * *

Mary Page knew and worked with Mickey at Oxford United for the best part of four decades and she summed this period of time up perfectly: 'Everyone was right. Every tribute to him was absolutely right. No exaggeration. He was just a one-off.' And whilst there is no escaping the profound tragedy of the situation, there is perhaps some comfort in that. 'Death,' as Stonesfield Strikers chairman Paul Charles put it, 'shone a wonderful light on his life.'

Chapter 27

What drove Mickey Lewis?

'For those on the outside, working in football looks terrifically exciting. There are plenty of times when that's true. But it can be a hell of a grind when results are patchy. And if you stay in the industry long enough, the game's cynical side can wear you down. [But for] Mickey the wide-eyed enthusiasm he had as a child kicking the ball around for the first time was undimmed.'

Oxford Mail journalist Mark Edwards

FOR A man whose passion for the game never dwindled, even during the more bruising experiences in a game and industry that became increasingly brutal across Mickey's career, there is a natural question that requires some attention: what drove and sustained Mickey Lewis? Or, to frame it slightly differently, how did he keep guaranteeing a performance and enjoying the occasion so consistently and for so long?

The most revealing period in which to explore this question comes from the years after Mickey stopped working with

Chris Wilder. After he left Oxford in 2014, Wilder made a remarkable ascent through the Football League and ultimately to the Premier League, while Mickey continued to work in and around the Oxfordshire area with sides further from the pinnacle of the professional game.

Whether or not there was an opportunity for Mickey to follow Wilder at the time of his departure for Northampton in 2014 is, as discussed earlier, open to conjecture and the differing memories from those there at the time. And we do not for a moment intend to suggest there was ever any sort of rift between the two men. They were and remained the firmest of friends from the moment they began working together to Mickey's passing and Wilder and his family remain close to Suzanne and Zach. Zach regularly visits Bramall Lane.

But considering the years after 2014 in Mickey's life and career, in which he dedicated himself primarily to young footballers in Oxfordshire, away from the glamour and the money of the modern game, is still revealing.

What did those years say about Mickey's nature as a manager and, perhaps more importantly, his priorities, his values and his character?

* * *

We can rule out any suggestion that Mickey wasn't fussed about success. Anecdotal evidence from Mickey's time as caretaker of Oxford United, as well as our own experiences playing under him, made that much clear. And failure certainly disturbed him.

Mark Edwards wrote a piece after Mickey's first caretaker spell in charge of Oxford United, around the turn of the millennium, considering why he hadn't got the job full-time. His conclusion? Mickey was simply too nice. He was everybody's mate. And that's great on the coaching staff, but not in the dugout. As Edwards put it: 'As a journalist, you were never going to have a drink with Alex Ferguson, but with Mickey you would have done.'

The day the piece was published in the paper, Mickey rang Edwards. He'd seen the article and wanted to discuss it over a beer. Edwards remembers the meeting as entirely amicable. Enjoyable, even. But Mickey certainly disagreed with what Edwards had written. In Edwards's eyes, this was a man who wanted the top job and who felt he'd basically been told he'd failed.

Of course, in typical Mickey fashion, he and Edwards shook hands at the end of their conversation and left without any bad blood. In fact, Edwards was so impressed with Mickey's parting words, he wrote them down and, so, was able to recount them verbatim over 20 years later.

'You have your job to do, Mark. I totally respect that. And I have mine to do. Whatever you write, even if I disagree, we won't fall out. Life's too short. We'll have a beer. We'll still be mates.'

But the sense of hurt that Edwards picked up in that conversation wasn't an isolated moment. Kelvin Thomas remembered the end of Mickey's time at Oxford the second time around as a period in which 'he wasn't as cheerful as you'd expect him to be'. For a man who seemed so adept at compartmentalising on-field struggled, this is probably a bigger revelation than it sounds. Mickey did feel burned by his inability to convert his caretaker spells into the top job at the club to which he'd dedicated so much of his life. After the second occasion, he was perhaps reluctant to put himself in another position where he could be knocked back again.

But any such reluctance surely wouldn't have kept Mickey down forever.

Given that Mickey was surely bothered about success and creating winning teams, perhaps then we can consider the two available paths that could feasibly have been ahead of Mickey in 2014 and beyond, if he'd plotted an ascent up the Football League: first-team management and coaching.

* * *

Martin Tyler stressed here the difference between first-team management and coaching. It is an increasingly important and binary distinction. 'Managers put a set of principles in place and that translates to the coaches who apply it. They're different skills.'

Tyler knows Chris Wilder well. In his view, Wilder's great skill is defining and communicating that common philosophy. That was at the heart of Sheffield United's success during their first surge into and up the Premier League. As Tyler sees it, it is the exact thing that has been lacking amongst all the talent and riches for Manchester United at Old Trafford.

So, taking first-team management first, why did things never really work out for Mickey as a number one, at least in the professional game?

Neither of Mickey's caretaker spells at Oxford, including the one following Wilder's departure, were deemed successful enough by the club to warrant a permanent contract. As much as the players and fans wanted Mickey to succeed on both occasions, he just couldn't put a run of wins together.

There were mitigating circumstances. On both occasions, there were financial difficulties, meaning Mickey had an exhausting task in front of him to keep spirits up and points flowing, without ever really having a squad capable of delivering the results fans and the board might have expected. Of course, navigating such situations was one of his great talents – 'it could be worse, it's only football' – but it wasn't a set of circumstances that lent themselves to a charge up the divisions.

Those two periods help explain Mickey's limited exposure as a number one and his limited work in the professional game after leaving Oxford for the last time in 2014. But such was his reputation that, assuming he did want to work in another professional dugout, these experiences surely shouldn't have been conclusive.

Kelvin Thomas wondered if there was a perception issue. This was all happening as football entered what we might call its Guardiola era. The touchline has increasingly become about sharp suits, performance analysts and real-time data feeds on iPads next to the water bottles and balls. The Tony Pulis baseball cap is out. 'That stuff filters down and has an impact on how clubs want to project themselves,' Thomas said.

And running, as he does, a professional football club, Thomas likely understands this dynamic more than most. As the game has become increasingly global and commercialised, and data has taken centre stage in the analysis and pursuit of high performance, the 'come on lads' approach to coaching and management that the Pulis baseball cap or the Mickey Lewis tracksuit has come to embody, fairly or otherwise, has gone increasingly out of fashion. That's not to suggest it's a golden rule – clubs have continued to reach for the emergency Neil Warnock button in the latter stages of recent seasons – but, generally speaking, boards and their fanbases are biased towards younger, more progressive, more scholarly appointments.

As the divide between the financial haves and have-nots grows larger – exacerbated as it is by parachute payments – clubs like Oxford and Thomas's Northampton perhaps see this route as one of the few avenues to finding an edge available to them within the constraints of the modern game. More and more lower-league clubs are searching for their Kieran McKenna in the hope of 'doing an Ipswich'. Des Buckingham is a perfect example of the trend.

So, by the early 2010s, Mickey was perhaps, despite all his talents, on the wrong side of this particular industry evolution.

But, in truth, there is another possibility that must be considered. Some of those we spoke to wondered if, in that curiously paradoxical way generally reserved for male-dominated industries, Mickey was too nice for the top job.

In a '42 Things About Chris Wilder' article for the *Oxford Mail* from September 2009, Wilder is asked if he sees himself working in the Premier League: 'I am ambitious and I would love to manage there.' He's then asked to describe himself in five words. He chooses amongst them 'selfish' and 'obsessive'. It's hard to imagine Mickey describing himself in the same way.

That's not to say he never had to drop players or that he wouldn't engage in some of the tougher elements of running football teams. He did so, often, including in the context of youth teams where big dreams were often at stake. He was also brave to give young players a break, even when he was under pressure. But no one we spoke to chose 'ruthless' as the word they felt best described Mickey. And ruthlessness is still perceived by many to be a vital component for a successful career in elite management.

'I've known a lot of managers who are ruthless,' Oxford United's Andy Whing remembered, 'in the way they speak to people, the way they've got this authority over people. They need people to follow them. Maybe Mickey was too nice. He would have struggled to let people down, to let players go, to drop players.'

Oxford City's Paul Lee talked about Mickey in exactly the same light:

'He never pissed anyone off. And you know why? He found it very hard to drop people. Even if it was his or partly his decision, he didn't want to ever let anybody down or disappoint anybody.'

That's a Mickey Lewis that we, too, recognise. In both of our tenures as captains of the university team, Mickey was careful regarding his involvement with team selection. He would tell Suzanne that it simply wasn't his role, that he knew the captain was in charge – which, according to the club's rules, he was. And it's possible that he wanted to give us real leadership experience, throwing us right into the lion's den of management. But for a man with such a tough exterior, it was always striking how he'd step away when those phone calls had to be made. Whing remembers that Wilder 'didn't have a problem with any of that'.

Sam Long was a youth player at Oxford United at the time of Wilder's tenure, sometimes travelling with the first team, and he put it more bluntly: 'Wilder was the one that would give you the bollocking. Mickey would be the one mopping up.'

So, Mickey was a players' coach, with a gift for recognising personalities, understanding individuals and pulling people up and together, usually with humour. That made him extremely valuable for a tough personality such as Wilder. But whilst Oxford Radio's Jerome Sale wondered if he didn't quite realise how talented he was, especially in terms of his emotional intelligence, there is also the possibility he just wasn't ruthless enough to succeed in a top job.

* * *

But even recognising all this, many of those interviewed for this book – including some who work in the professional game today – were still quick to stress that Mickey was, and would still be, a standout coach. An assistant. A number two.

Out of everyone we spoke to, Wilder has surely had the most successful career in the dugout since those heady days at the Kassam back in the late noughties and early 2010s, and he stressed how much he trusted Mickey's eye and valued his opinion long after they'd stopped sharing a dugout. And the philosophy they shared remains a key part of how Wilder views his approach to football, even applying it as he did to life in the Premier League: 'Be aggressive, be committed, go out there to win and if you don't, then move on to the next one.'

Given the pace of Des Buckingham's ascent to Championship management, a similar assessment of Mickey's skill seems particularly credible coming from him:

> 'I think he would have thrived in today's game. There have never been many like him, but there are few of that type of character and coach now. Especially in the youth spaces. Lots of people can forget to be themselves nowadays.'

But given Wilder and Buckingham's especially close personal relationship to Mickey, it's worth noting, too, that they weren't the only ones to champion Mickey's enduring skill as a coach. Whether from Ross Weatherstone, Sam Long or Paul Lee, who has worked as a scout at Fulham, the message was the same. Whilst Mickey would certainly have had to adapt to the new personalities and dressing-room atmospheres in football today – 'it's a bit more sensitive, nowadays', as Long put it – he had all the attributes of a top-level coach.

So why then did Mickey's coaching career not take him on a path towards the upper echelons and the riches of England's top tiers? Why was he never the Premier League or Championship coach, assistant or even youth team boss that so many said he could and should have been?

* * *

Outstanding skill, especially with people, and the work ethic to prepare properly to be successful, and win the game in front of you are important qualities. But career ambition is another and that's a distinction that perhaps holds a key to understanding why Mickey, having left Oxford United, ultimately remained in Oxfordshire for the rest of his life.

Tristan tested this on more than one occasion, asking Mickey whenever he came back glowing from weekends he'd spent with Zach visiting Wilder in Sheffield why he wasn't up there with him, why he wasn't having that conversation with Wilder? But he just didn't want to do that. 'He was the best football man I've ever met, but in his professional capacity, he just never really pushed the button.'

'I didn't see any of that [ambition] in him, really,' echoed team-mate Phil Gilchrist. 'You see some people posturing, getting ready to move on, for the next opportunity, but Mickey was just totally loyal to the job he was doing.'

And it wasn't only loyalty to the job for Mickey. It was also loyalty to a place. Oxford, since that move from Derby way back in the 1980s, had become home and a place to set down deep roots. Aside from that short period in Des Moines, the season in Doncaster and a few other fleeting stints elsewhere, the quiet villages of Oxfordshire and the vibrant atmosphere of its centre had, by the time of Wilder's move to Northampton, been the setting of Mickey's life for over 20 years.

The pubs in Woodstock were his second living room, the streets of the city centre were a stomping ground with memories at every turn and the parks were a playground for his little boy, Zach.

And the place had a great affection for him, too. During a university training session in University Parks in 2018, one of the authors went away from the pitch to fetch a ball. A starry-eyed dog walker stopped him: 'Excuse me, but is that Mickey Lewis?' On receiving confirmation it was, the man walked off into the distance, smiling to himself: 'What a legend.'

Part of Mickey's loyalty to place was loyalty to family, too.

Andy Whing once tried to get Mickey to join him at Banbury, as an assistant or a director of football. Whing wanted to learn from him, to 'have a solid character around'. But Zach was young and Mickey felt his work–life balance would have been affected. So, he turned Whing down.

Tristan Lewis echoed Whing as he remembered a man for whom being a husband and a dad came before everything:

'Working in football is completely boisterous. No one, especially back when we were working together, really talked about their feelings or their family. It was about shagging, drinking and football. But Mick, when he had Zach, you saw the joy in his face when he spoke about him. If Suzy was phoning – and his phone was always on loud, never on fucking silent – he'd stop, he'd take the call.

'When he learned how to use FaceTime, you'd hear him shouting at Zach, even though Zach couldn't fucking talk. It was never not cool to talk about family with Mick. It was a totally different, alternative view on life and the importance of what we were doing.'

And that was exactly how Adam Everitt remembered Mickey's priorities, too. Everitt was club captain during Mickey's spell at Hayes & Yeading. He was the senior player. So, naturally, he and Mickey gravitated towards each other, particularly for their pre-match cup of tea. And what did they talk about? 'I never heard him say a single thing about his career,' said Everitt. 'He'd just say "Ah, different lifetime, mate."' They'd soon be talking about life and about family. 'I've never had a relationship like that with any other manager or coach.'

And so, leaving Oxfordshire for a nomadic life at the grindstone of the professional game felt a bridge – or motorway – too far for Mickey. Just as he essentially became a one-club man as a player, he was a one-city man as a coach and a happy man for it.

In local journalist David Pritchard's eyes: 'Football was his life, but it almost didn't matter who it was. He found the pleasure in improving the players, whatever the level.'

'Perhaps,' Pritchard mused, 'that was enough for him.'

* * *

And there was not even the slightest hint from anyone we spoke with that Mickey was ever jealous, even as his old friend Wilder drew Premier League plaudits and became a much-lauded manager at football's top table.

Close friend Kelvin Thomas and wife Suzanne both remembered how proud Mickey was of what Wilder and, indeed, all of his friends achieved. And that was all borne out in his actions, too. Whenever Mickey and Zach went up to Sheffield, Mickey and Wilder would have a beer in the manager's office after the game – from a fully-stocked fridge, no doubt. When Sheffield United were down in London for a match against Queens Park Rangers, Mickey arranged somewhere for them to train. Outside of the season, the families continued to meet up regularly, not just former close colleagues but genuine friends.

So, from understanding that, there remains one final question to answer about Mickey Lewis: What is his legacy?

Chapter 28

Legacy?

'To find the best in others;
To leave the world a bit better …
To know even one life has breathed
easier because you have lived.
This is to have succeeded.'

What is Success? [abridged]

by Ralph Waldo Emerson
Read at Mickey's funeral by Steve Gwilym

SO, MICKEY never made it to the Premier League.

But that is not the secret to answering the question of his legacy. Conventional metrics of success rarely are. That is why the comedian Jim Carrey once said that his biggest wish was for everybody to achieve their dreams, so everyone could then realise that doing so wasn't the secret to a long and contented life.

We would argue instead that Mickey's legacy is found in the very qualities that perhaps made it harder for him to reach the sharpest ends of the increasingly ruthless industry in which he worked. That is, his legacy lies in the enduring influence of the life he built around his deep affection and loyalty to place and people, his unshakeable commitment to family and his passion and skill for working with and developing young players, particularly away from the glamour and grind of the professional game.

In this book, we have distilled this approach to life into four of the adages of which Mickey was always so fond and which in their entirety comprise an enviable philosophy.

First there is *guaranteeing a performance.*

As Mark Edwards put it, it was how Mickey played, coached and lived his life:

> 'My first memory is as a fan of Oxford United and seeing this mad midfielder charge around the pitch, kicking everyone and everything. I'm sure he'd agree he was never the finest midfielder, he wasn't spraying passes here and there, but nobody would beat him in desire, passion and will to win. I couldn't help but notice, for how he played the game. That was how he lived his life.'

And thanks to Mickey, it is how so many who had the pleasure of knowing him try to play, coach and live now, too.

There are all those who regularly recall Mickey's voice encouraging them: *Don't let it pass you by.* A piece of wisdom that he used to remind himself and those around him – especially the young players in his care – that life passes quickly and that the power to shape it is in your hands.

Most who knew Mickey hold with them his commitment to *enjoying the occasion*, too. In doing so, they are remembering that no win or milestone, personal or professional, is complete without a glass raised to soak it in, break it down and get excited for the next one. And every trial, tribulation or achievement is only truly worthwhile if you can go through it with family and with friends. Indeed, Mickey's enduring love for people, and the way in which he brought out the best in those around him and every room he was in, was perhaps the quality that defined him above all else and which continues to inspire so many.

And then, finally, there's having *one for the road*, as we've just explored, which was, for Mickey, an expression of interest in and dedication to other people. Mickey certainly knew that the extra hour you spend in the pub might be the hour you remember years later and that remains true for so many who knew him.

So this – all these adages and approaches to life, the guiding philosophy they represent and the way in which so many people carry all that forward with them – is the essence of Mickey's legacy.

But throughout this book we have tried to tell Mickey's story through the eyes and memories of all those who gave a significant amount of time and emotion to being interviewed, as much as our own. So, for the final time, we would ask that you don't just take our word for it.

Consider instead the people who laughed and cried as they recalled a career of crunching tackles, once-a-season screamers, eye-watering team talks and brilliant stories starting in the centre circle and ending at the pub or in a Spanish fountain.

People like Oxford Radio's Jerome Sale, who went as far as to wonder whether Mickey's legacy is intimately intertwined with the very existence of Oxford United today. 'I genuinely wonder, without characters like Mickey, and there really weren't many of them,' Sale said to us, 'whether Oxford United still exists. There were some really dark times. But Mickey made them feel less dark.' That same feeling led lifelong fan Phil Chambers to credit Mickey with laying the foundations for the success the club are enjoying today.

People who told us that so much of their careers today – including Des Buckingham, Paul Wanless and James Constable, who have had long careers in football – are a result of the experiences they had and the lessons they learned under Mickey's stewardship.

'He made a massive difference to my time at the club and my career,' was how Constable started. Before continuing:

'And I take bits of how Mickey was to help the next generation of players coming through. His nature. His personality. His arm round the shoulder. In many ways, he was ahead of his time, working on the players away from football, giving them that freedom on the football pitch, by taking away the pressures off it.'

People like Mickey's brother, Peter, who still does his best to live Mickey's philosophy: 'He taught me to work hard and just enjoy absolutely everything.' And people like the young man who learned that there is no shame in expressing love for your family and taking a call from your wife during a busy work day, even in an industry that for too long has been masculine and emotionally underdeveloped. Or the countless players who learned that the game was about the friends you make along the way. Or the nervous university students who learned that to be your own man, to accept yourself and work from there, is the best route to a life well-lived.

People, to put it simply, for whom Mickey was such a singular and memorable influence that they often spoke to us as if he was still right there with us in the room.

Nowhere was that more true than with Jules Austin, the quiet, deep-thinking member of one of Mickey's earlier university sides. A video message he sent to Mickey following the news of his cancer diagnosis captured the guiding quality of Mickey's philosophy and approach to life, and the lasting impact Mickey has had on thousands of people, perhaps better than anyone else.

'I just looked at the last messages we'd exchanged. Yours just said "Keep playing, you can't beat it."'

If there's a single message to take from this book, if there's a single message to take from Mickey's life, it's that.

Keep playing. Just like Mickey would have done.

You really can't beat it.

Authors' Note

WE HAVE tried throughout this book to ensure that our voices are not at its centre. Mickey's story was shaped and shared by too many people, in many instances well before we were both even born, for us to do that.

But we do want to leave you with a clear sense of why we wanted, and why we felt so honoured, to bring Mickey's story together into *Mad Dog* and to bring the book out into the world.

We thought it made sense then to finish this project by asking each other to reflect on our own relationships with Mickey, both of which played out in the later years of his life, thanks to our respective involvement in the University of Oxford Football Club.

Alex started by remembering his first year at university, during which he was part of the second team. The squad used to train on Friday nights at the same time as the first team, the Blues. Everyone in that second team wanted to be on the other side of the training pitch and there was one main reason for that: Mickey Lewis. Whether he was flying around in the rondo with them at the start of the session or barking at them to run their sprints harder whilst they reflected on that Wednesday's loss, he was clearly a coach and a man that everyone wanted to be around. His was a team everyone badly wanted to be a part of.

Alex's first real conversation with Mickey was on the side of the pre-season training pitch before the following season, as he lay on the floor with cramp. 'What's the matter, son?' That was Mickey. 'Ah, well, you see Mickey, I flew back in from Thailand last night. I spent a few weeks there over the summer. I've just got a bit of cramp.' Mickey laughed and moved on. It perhaps should have been obvious then, from the twinkle in his eye as he chuckled at the fishbowl-induced lack of fitness, that Mickey was a man who took enjoying the occasion as seriously as he did playing the game.

In 2017, Alex became the captain of the first team and he distinctly remembers being sat at home during the summer staring at his home phone, which Mickey had promised to ring at any moment, wondering what he could possibly have to add by way of insight or leadership to a man entering the fourth decade of his remarkable footballing career? But it was in such situations that Mickey's genius – and we truly think it was genius – shone through more than anywhere else.

In that call and through that year, Alex saw up close the extent to which Mickey respected and trusted those around him, by demanding the highest standards from them but never creating the negative energy or fear of failure that can so often come with that. He provided the wisdom and perspective of a long career, especially after losses, after which Alex remembers avoiding Mickey's calls for a day or so, before eventually receiving a voicemail. 'You can't hide forever, son, it's time we move on to the next one.'

When thinking about the hours a week spent on the phone plotting a way through the season, Alex recalls Mickey asking questions, listening and then backing to the hilt whatever decision it was he was making. Thinking of that old cliche, Alex was one of many who would have run through a brick wall for Mickey, because Mickey gave people the sense he'd have run through it for them, too.

Some of the squad would sometimes go back to watch games in the years that followed that season. There's a paragraph in one of our favourite sports books, *Friday Night Lights*, that talks about that exact phenomenon, when players return and 'paw around the edge of the pandemonium', getting a big hug from an old coach who quickly moves on to more important things and seeing an air of invincibility that was once theirs now belonging to someone else. That was never the case with these trips back. In fact, Alex's last memory of seeing Mickey in person was the two of them sitting in the dugout long after a match had finished, as the floodlights were slowly winding down, talking about football and about life.

Leo's picture is similar. He remembers one of the very first encounters he had with Mickey and the way it set the tone for the impact he would go on to have on his life.

After having informed Mickey that he would be the new captain of the university first XI for the coming season, Mickey invited Leo to have a coffee in Summertown, just north of central Oxford, in the summer of 2018.

Leo remembers being bloody nervous. The armband for the university side came with a set of responsibilities that, as a second-year student, younger than most of the players he'd be captaining, he felt a little unprepared for. He felt he could manage organising the training sessions, who washed the kit and how we would travel to matches. But the captain also had to pick the team, which meant each Tuesday he would be calling up his mates to tell them why he'd instead selected their best mate or their enemy who was now going out with their ex-girlfriend.

As Leo thinks back to arriving at Costa Coffee for that meeting, he remembers sweating and it wasn't at all warm. He hopped off his bike and checked his watch. Three minutes late. Fuck, he thought. A detail that undermines everything that follows. He saw Mickey inside, drinking from a mug that could fit a newborn kitten. Better get the fuck in there, he thought, before Mickey gets bored and asks last year's skipper to do another degree.

Fumbling through his pockets to make sure he had enough change for a coffee, he pushed open the door and made his way to him. The two of them shook hands and, out of politeness (having seen his coffee), Leo asked if he wanted another drink.

'Large triple latte mate, with an extra shot.'

It was 5.30pm.

Leo grabbed the coffee and sat back down, leather notebook in his sweaty palms, ready to share his rookie tactical ideas with a man who had played and managed in the game for over 30 years, winning at Wembley and overseeing an unparalleled record of Oxford–Cambridge Varsity wins.

Mickey clearly saw the nervousness in Leo's eyes. He must have, because he grasped his rocket fuel in his right hand, flashed his eyes open wide and said something that has always stuck.

'Don't worry, son. Be your own man and everything is going to be fine.'

Those words are written on a card that Leo will forever keep in his wallet.

* * *

Just like so many of the memories and anecdotes that people shared with us, it's clear from both sets of reflections here that Mickey brought all of himself – in a way that was so consistent – to every interaction and relationship he formed.

Irrespective of age or experience, he met people on a level, with a respect and a sense of mischief that meant you listened to him and learned from him all the time, enjoying the experience immensely as you did.

So, we hope that in the pages of this book we've captured the Mickey you knew. Or if you didn't know him, that you now feel like you did. We hope that you've felt the love and respect we and so many others did in playing for, working with and knowing Mickey. And we hope there are lessons to be taken from Mickey's story, too.

Mickey knew that he couldn't guarantee his legacy, just like he couldn't guarantee a result. But he certainly could guarantee how he treated others, how he approached every match and how he shared his experience with younger players. And if we have learned one thing from Mickey, it is that how you behave towards others will become the measure of your character after you are gone.

So, perhaps, next time you find yourself looking for answers, it's Mickey's gruff Midlands voice in your ear, repeating one of his famous lines.

'You *can* guarantee a performance.'

'Don't let it pass you by.'

'Enjoy the occasion.'

'And come on, mate, just have one for the road.'

London.

September 2024.

Acknowledgements

MAD DOG is our first book and we only knew Mickey for a relatively small portion of his life. This story simply wouldn't exist, therefore, if it wasn't for the help, support and guidance we've received from a great many people.

Firstly, we want to thank all the people who spoke to us for this book.

There were several people who knew Mickey particularly well and who were willing to speak at great length. Broadcasting legend Jim Rosenthal took the time to meet us for lunch right before he had to get to Brentford for a 3pm kick-off. Jim's wisdom and his enduring enthusiasm for the game was obvious, as was his love for Mickey. He also took time to provide us with guiding comments for the introduction. And former Oxford United executive and current Northampton Town chairman Kelvin Thomas spoke at equally generous length from Florida, offering his help wherever we needed it, including reading a draft of the book. His main correction was that he was a slip fielder, more than a bowler.

A few of the current members of staff and those associated with some of Mickey's former clubs helped us along with their own stories, fact-checking and club photographs – particular thanks here to the likes of Des Buckingham, Chris Williams, Laurie Rampling and Martin Brodetsky.

There was also a flood of tributes from across the University of Oxford football community that followed on from the announcement of Mickey's illness and then his passing. Many of these were gathered together back in 2021, to send to Mickey, and we leaned heavily on that document for certain sections here. So, we're grateful to everyone who contributed to that – particularly to Jules Austin, whose words provided us with the perfect way to end the book, and who is in our thoughts – for their input but also their part in a community which we both hold incredibly dear. We're also particularly grateful here to Ben Putland, Mark Addley, Brendan McGurk et al, and Leon Farr, for their thoughtful contributions.

And we are also incredibly grateful to all the following people who agreed to be interviewed for or contribute to the book, listed here in alphabetical order:

Mike Adamson
Craig Adey
Martin Allen
Ron Atkinson
Dan Bond
Mick Brown
James Constable

Phil Chambers

Paul Charles

Malcolm Crosby

Eddie Denton

Peter Drury

Mark Edwards

Adam Everitt

Peter Frain

Phil Gilchrist

Mark Grew

Phil Heath

Brian Horton

Mark Lawrenson

Paul Lee

Tristan Lewis

Sam Long

Jim Magilton

Ian Matthews

Andy Melville

Mick Moore

David Moss

Jon Murray

Stuart Nelson

Mary Page

Dave Penney

David Pritchard

James Redmayne

Ally Robertson

Les Robinson

Anton Rogan

Jerome Sale

Denis Smith

Geoff Snape

Les Taylor

Martin Tyler

Paul Wanless

Ross Weatherstone

Andy Whing

Chris Wilder

Thanks also to the football fans up and down the country who do such painstakingly detailed work on fan forums and websites like *yellowsforum.co.uk* and *toffeeweb.com*, which were invaluable as we pieced together the details of Mickey's career.

Of course, all the interviews and research in the world do not make a book.

So, secondly, thank you to the handful of people who sat with our drafts for hours and gave us invaluable feedback. Thanks, in particular, to our parents, Tim Willems, and Martin Hitchcock, without whom this book would have been a much paler imitation of what you have in your hands now.

Thank you also to the team at Pitch Publishing – including Ian Passingham, Dean Rockett and Duncan Olner for believing in Mickey's story and bringing this book into the world.

And, of course, we are so thankful to you for buying the book and playing your own part in celebrating Mickey's life and keeping his legacy alive.

Finally, and most importantly of all, thank you to Suzanne Lewis, who has been the foundation stone for this project. She was the person who trusted us to tell Mickey's story and sent us on our way with gusto when we came to her with a half-baked idea a couple of years ago. Since then, with the help of our well-used joint WhatsApp group, she has provided us with names and numbers to arrange interviews, as well as newspaper cuttings and other memorabilia from across Mickey's life and career. She has read several drafts of the book. She gave us the freedom we needed to tell this story and kept us on the right track whenever we needed it.

As per Suzanne's choosing, the wonderful charity See Saw, which provides grief support for children and young people in the Oxfordshire area, will receive any and all of the proceeds generated by sales of this book. You can learn more about their work at their website, *www.seesaw.org.uk*.

Thank you to Mickey's brothers, Steve and Peter, who were equally generous in how they shared with us their time, memories and anecdotes.

Thank you to Mickey's son, Zach – who is already a better footballer and cricketer than both of us – who was one of our primary inspirations for starting and then eventually finishing this book. He also read our drafts and his comments and suggestions were the wisest of the lot.

And, finally, thank you to Mickey Lewis. For everything.

Appendix I

*University of Oxford captain (2020/21) Ben
Putland's funeral tribute to Mickey Lewis*

HI ALL. For those that don't know me, I'm Ben, the University of Oxford's 'Blues' football captain this year or, as Mickey called me, 'Mr Covid Officer'. Suzanne, I'd just like to start by saying a huge thank you for asking me to say a few words today.

I feel honoured and privileged to be up here and, as you know, I'm not just speaking about Mickey from my perspective, but I'm also speaking for 18 generations of Blues players that Mickey's coached over his nearly two decades with the club and there's a little piece of everyone's thoughts in this speech.

The fact that all those generations came together to send a book of messages to Mickey, you and Zach shows how much of a lasting impact he's had on our lives.

If times were different, they'd all be here today, along with an army of football clubs, friends and family, but instead I know they're all watching from home sending a huge amount of love and support.

Mickey joined the university football club in 2002 and since then he's coached hundreds of players four days a week on Mondays, Wednesdays, Fridays and Sundays. Our matchdays were on Wednesdays and they were the absolute highlight of our week.

After sprinting out of lectures, and locking up our bikes, we piled into the changing rooms, buzzing for the game, fighting over the last pair of socks that hadn't shrunk in the dryer. There was always music blaring in the background and if Mickey got his way, it would usually be some Barry White.

And before the warm-up, we'd all be looking forward to his team talk.

He always knew what to say: reminding everyone of their duties; the game plan; instilling confidence, but never arrogance; getting us up for the game to the point we'd be listening silently but bouncing off the walls with nervousness and excitement.

Then the game kicks off and Mickey's voice is obviously the loudest, so loud you could hear him from St Clements roundabout!

Always words of encouragement, like 'FASTER' because we're moving the ball too slow around defence.

Or 'GO' as he's signalling us to start the high press.

Or, as became common in recent years, 'PASS THE BALL DOMMY!' Because despite coaching him for five years, Mickey never quite persuaded Dom to pass the ball.

And after the game he'd *always* encourage us to go out and celebrate with a few drinks. He'd been known to join a few nights out, too, drinking the famous Vinnies Pinky, which has five shots of vodka. Apparently, he used to follow them with Stella chasers, then stumble over to Park End before spending 45 minutes trying to find the exit.

But those team nights out would come back to bite the captains in the morning, because Mickey had a cruel habit of calling bright and early at 7am to chat about the game the day before.

He knew what he was doing and, of course, the captains answered every single time! Except me, I got lucky because all the nightclubs were closed this year.

Mickey's brilliant coaching was responsible for what can only be described as the most successful period in the university football club's modern history.

He led the team to five league titles, most recently the BUCS Midlands Division 1A last season, which, for many of us, was the best year of football we'd ever had.

He won five of the eight Varsity Matches against our local rivals, Oxford Brookes.

And then there was the big one, the occasion I think he looked forward to the most, the Oxford versus Cambridge Varsity Match at the end of the season.

For those that don't know, there's not a lot of love between us and 'the Tabs' and Mickey knew that. In fact, I think he felt it and much of the year was spent reminding us about the game, preparing us mentally and ramping up training as the date got closer.

And, luckily for us, he got pretty good at beating them. Losing only three games inside 90 minutes, winning at Craven

Cottage, the Kassam, The Hive, Selhurst Park and the Abbey Stadium.

Those Cambridge teams must have been the only people on the planet to dread the sight of Mickey Lewis. At least these days, anyway. Travel back to the 1980s and I bet we'd find a few more that were on the receiving end of some of his tackles!

But Mickey was more than just about winning, too. He got what it means to every individual to get their Blue. You have to actually get on to the pitch during a Varsity Match to get your Blue and Mickey worked out at the start of his time with the club that getting a Blue meant much more than just football. Before the Varsity Match, he would work out who was in their last year at the university so he could make sure they got on the pitch. I even heard of goalkeepers being subbed on at left-back when Oxford were up 1-0 in a tight match!

Like he did at many clubs, Mickey drove our culture of hard work and determination, working us hard in every training session until we were knackered.

But more than anything, he had an incredible ability to make everything fun. He brightened your day with his infectious enthusiasm for life and he made sure everyone went home with a warm glow of happiness and satisfaction.

To quote Pat Collins, our captain in 2019/20: 'It was the way [he] ran the training sessions but not even that, it's just the way [he was].' It's true. Training was as much about seeing Mickey as it was about kicking the ball. He made you forget about everything when you were in his company.

And those training sessions on the 3G were some of the best times of our lives. They'll stick with the young Blues as much as they've stuck with the old.

The times when he broke into a sprint pointing towards the box but shouted 'LAST MAN IN THE CENTRE CIRCLE!' fooling half the team and chuckling to himself every time. He always made sure to remind us that the Oxford boys fell for this more than the young lads he coached midweek.

Or the times when we'd be playing a game like piggy-in-the-middle called 'rondo'. Mickey used to sneak in beside someone and then, before you knew it, the ball's at his feet, he's buckled at the knees and you think he's going to fall over but, with a little touch with the outside of his boot, he still manages to nutmeg someone, hobbling off in celebration, everyone going crazy.

They were the best times.

I know Mickey is not only a legend at Oxford University, but he's also a legend at Oxford City, Oxford United, Stonesfield Strikers and the many other clubs he's been involved in over the years, and everything I'm saying today probably echoes through those teams, too.

He had a passion for coaching, particularly young people. And many of the qualities that made him a great footballer made him a brilliant coach: his commitment, his determination to work hard no matter what, his unrelenting passion for football and his unwavering positivity. He just made you fall in love with the game all over again.

And during all of the years in his coaching, he never made a negative comment to any player – and we had *a lot* of average players over the years that must have frustrated him at times!

But not only was Mickey a brilliant coach, he was also our role model and many of the lessons he taught went beyond football – preparing us for life, helping us in job interviews but, ultimately, making everyone better people.

He didn't sit there and tell us how to be better team-mates, better leaders, how to be more positive and optimistic, because he didn't need to. He showed you.

And that was the beauty of Mickey. You absorbed it without thinking but if you thought about it, you learnt so much more. He taught us what it meant to value hard work, to put our trust and loyalty into others to become and achieve something bigger than ourselves. He taught us to never let it pass you by, to seize the moment, to help others, to be warm, kind, generous, humble, funny and, above all, to passionately enjoy what you're doing.

And what made him extra special was that he wasn't all of these words to just one person or a mixture to different people, but that he was all of these things to everyone. He treated everyone the same and we are so lucky to have had him.

So, Mick – on behalf of the thousands of friends you've made over the years – thank you for everything.

Appendix II

'Chairman's Message to Our Young Players', from
Stonesfield Strikers chairman Paul Charles

I WANTED to write to you because I know just how much you adored having Mickey as a coach.

When someone important in your life dies, there's often a lot to take in. When someone dies, we may feel lots of different emotions or sometimes nothing at all. And when someone dies suddenly, when we weren't expecting it, our feelings can be even more jumbled. You might be sad, okay, confused, scared, calm, anxious, angry. Maybe you have some other feelings. However you feel, the important thing to remember is that you may experience loads of new emotions. This is a natural part of grief.

Most people who have had someone special die have good days and bad days. It's okay to have a cry and it's still okay to have fun sometimes. You don't have to be sad all the time and having fun doesn't mean that you love that special person any less.

Try to remember that you're not alone – family and friends are there to support you. Try talking with friends or family or your team coach about how you are feeling. You could each share your memories about Mickey; maybe even laugh and cry together. But if you do need more help, don't be afraid to ask.

The important thing to remember is that Mickey loved coaching you and being a big part of our club. I know Mickey wants you – all of us – to play on and to have fun! We'll soon be able to play football again and we'll find lots of ways to celebrate Mickey's life. Until then, if you have something you'd like our club to do to honour Mickey, then do let me know.

I'm looking forward to seeing you back playing soon.

Paul Charles, Chairman
Stonesfield Strikers FC